Ralph Eugene Meatyard

Ralph Eugene Meatyard

An American Visionary

Edited by
Barbara Tannenbaum

Essays by
Barbara Tannenbaum
David L. Jacobs
Van Deren Coke
Wendell Berry

Akron Art Museum, Ohio
Rizzoli, New York

This publication accompanies an exhibition of the same title organized by the Akron Art
Museum and selected by Barbara Tannenbaum and David L. Jacobs. The project was supported in
part by The Andy Warhol Foundation for the Visual Arts, Inc.; the National Endowment for the Arts, a federal
agency; the Mirapaul Foundation, Akron, Ohio; and one anonymous donor.

Exhibition Tour

San Francisco Museum of Modern Art
San Francisco, California
September 6–November 10, 1991

Oklahoma City Art Museum
Oklahoma City, Oklahoma
December 8, 1991–February 12, 1992

National Museum of American Art, Smithsonian Institution
Washington, D.C.
July 3–September 27, 1992

Newport Harbor Art Museum
Newport Beach, California
December 18, 1992–February 14, 1993

Akron Art Museum
Akron, Ohio
June 19–August 15, 1993

First published in the United States of America
in 1991 by Rizzoli International Publications, Inc.
300 Park Avenue South, New York, NY 10010

"Ralph Eugene Meatyard" by Van Deren Coke was originally
published in *Portfolio Three: Ralph Eugene Meatyard,* produced by
the Center for Photographic Studies, Louisville, Kentucky, 1974.

Library of Congress Cataloging-in-Publication Data

Meatyard, Ralph Eugene, 1925–1972.
Ralph Eugene Meatyard : an American visionary / edited by Barbara
Tannenbaum ; essays by Wendell Berry . . . [et al.].
    p. cm.
Includes bibliographical references.
ISBN 0-8478-1374-6. —ISBN 0-8478-1375-4 (pbk.)
1. Meatyard, Ralph Eugene, 1925–1972—Exhibitions.
2. Photography, Artistic—Exhibitions. I. Tannenbaum, Barbara.
II. Berry, Wendell, 1934–   III. Akron Art Museum. IV. Title.
TR647.M393 1991   779'.092—dc20   90-27651   CIP

Front cover: Romance (N.) From Ambrose Bierce #3, 1962
Back cover: Cemetery #32 [Double portrait on gravestone], 1960
Frontispiece: Untitled [Arched doorway with ghost], 1966

Designed by Steven Schoenfelder
Duotone separations made by Robert Hennessey
Composed by Graphic Composition, Inc., Athens, Georgia
Printed and bound by la cromolito, Milan, Italy

Contents

Foreword

It has been almost two decades since the art of Ralph Eugene Meatyard was published in a significant way, and the time for reappraisal of his visionary work is overdue. The text of this book, which accompanies a major retrospective exhibition of Meatyard's photography, chronicles the development of his work biographically and also places it in the context of American photographic history since World War II. During Meatyard's artistic maturity, photography critics were not especially receptive to his mystical and metaphorical approach to photography. Attention was then focused mostly on street photography, inspired by Robert Frank's seminal work, or on formalist studies that continued in the tradition of Paul Strand and Harry Callahan.

Compared to the 1960s, our own decade is more interested in several of Meatyard's primary concerns: his posed tableaux, his cultivation of multiple readings for his work, and his self-conscious definition of photography's unique characteristics as well as its reciprocal relationship with painting. But Meatyard is not a postmodernist in today's terminology, for his aesthetic quest was not characterized by aloofness and a lack of belief in the transcendent nature of art. Quite the opposite, in fact.

Most of the existing writing on the artist was undertaken within five years of his death in 1972, when the sense of loss was strong and the work itself still seemed tied to its maker. It is time now for a new analysis to be undertaken by scholars whose insights are different from those of Meatyard's colleagues and friends. It would, however, be foolish to ignore the unique perspective of those who collaborated with Meatyard, as distance and intimacy each have their advantages. This volume therefore includes writings by the exhibition's two curators who look at Meatyard's work with fresh eyes, Barbara Tannenbaum and David L. Jacobs, as well as two essays by those who knew the artist well, Van Deren Coke and Wendell Berry. Mirroring Meatyard's own diverse interests, these four writers approach his work from their different backgrounds in photography, art history, and literature.

It is a pleasure to thank funders and colleagues for supporting this exhibition and publication. Initial funding from the National Endowment for the Arts was a cornerstone without which this project could not have proceeded. Additional support from two Akron sources was especially meaningful: I thank the Mirapaul Foundation and its trustees Walter, Evan, and Matthew Mirapaul, and one anonymous donor. The High Museum of Art, the National Museum of American Art, the Newport Harbor Art Museum, and the Oklahoma City Art Museum have all been enthusiastic participants in this project. I am especially delighted that the premiere of the exhibition was hosted by the distinguished Department of Photography at the San Francisco Museum of Modern Art, whose curators have been longtime advocates of Meatyard's work.

For many years Akron Art Museum Curator Barbara Tannenbaum and I have admired Ralph Eugene Meatyard's photographs. In 1987, having heard that Meatyard's heirs were seeking a repository for the photographer's archives, we met with Meatyard's friend and fellow photographer Charles Traub and with Meatyard's son Christopher. The result of that meeting is this publication and its accompanying exhibition, both of which have come to fruition due to Barbara Tannenbaum's keen insight and intense dedication.

Mitchell D. Kahan
Director, Akron Art Museum

Acknowledgments

This project is the result of many people's efforts and generosity. I am deeply grateful to Christopher and Diane Meatyard. Neither the exhibition nor the book would have been possible without their assistance and their capable organization of the Meatyard archives. In addition to opening their home to the repeated and prolonged presence of two curators, they have generously lent most of the photographs in this exhibition. Two other lenders, Jonathan Greene and the University Photographic Archives, University of Louisville, also share our gratitude and appreciation.

I am indebted to co-curator and essayist David L. Jacobs, chairman of the Department of Art, University of Houston, for making collaboration a joyful, exciting process of companionship and intellectual exchange. At the San Francisco Museum of Modern Art, Sandra Phillips, curator of photography, Barbara Levine, exhibitions coordinator, and David Brown deserve recognition for their contributions. Diana C. du Pont, formerly assistant curator of photography at the San Francisco Museum of Modern Art and now curator of the University Art Museum, California State Museum, Long Beach, was involved with and committed to the exhibition from the beginning. Miriam Roberts, a free-lance curator, did a splendid job of amplifying and completing David Brown's initial work on the back matter. For the two wonderful memoirs of Meatyard in this volume I would like to express my gratitude to Wendell Berry and Van Deren Coke.

A number of Meatyard's relatives and friends generously shared their time and recollections to help us understand him as a person and an artist: Wendell and Tanya Berry, Bonnie Jean Cox, Guy Davenport, Jonathan Greene, James Baker Hall, Robert C. May, Christopher and Diane Meatyard, Madelyn Meatyard, Melissa Meatyard, Guy Mendes, Thomas Meyer, Charles Traub, and Jonathan Williams. We are deeply grateful to them for their help. Shelby Lee Adams, Andrew Borowiec, Lorraine Ferguson, Penny Rakoff, and Adam Weinberg provided technical information and pointed me toward rewarding resources. Several colleagues kindly agreed to read the two essays. We thank Van Deren Coke, Sheryl Conkelton, Nathan Lyons, Thomas Southall, and Barbara Frink for their thoughtful readings and suggestions. Any errors that remain are the responsibility of the authors, not of these readers.

The following individuals and institutions responded generously and promptly to our requests for information and assistance: the Akron-Summit County Public Library; Thomas Southall, curator of photography, the Amon Carter Museum; the libraries and Department of Photography of The Art Institute of Chicago; Amy Rule and Leslie Calmes of the Archives, Center for Creative Photography, The University of Arizona; Carol Ehlers, Ehlers Caudill Gallery; the Grunwald Center for the Graphic Arts, University of California, Los Angeles; Paul M. Hertzmann, Paul M. Hertzmann, Inc.; Judith Richards, Independent Curators, Incorporated; Andrew Eskind and Greg Drake, International Museum of Photography at George Eastman House; Louisville Courier-Journal; Print Study Room, The Metropolitan Museum of Art, New York; Department of Photography, Museum of Fine Arts, Houston; Clara Keyes, Morehead State College, Kentucky; Tony Troncale, Photo Study Center, The Museum of Modern Art, New York; Marcy Grassick, Division of Photographic History, and David Haberstich, Archives Center, National Museum of American History, Smithsonian Institution; Jeffrey Weidman, Clarence Ward Art Library, Oberlin College; Terry Stull, Photographic Society of America, Oklahoma City; Maria Pellerano, Archives, Princeton University Art Museum; Karen Brungardt, library assistant, San Francisco Museum of Modern Art; Cheryl Barton, Norton Simon Museum; Ann Gilbert, art librarian, University of California, Berkeley; James D. Birchfield, assistant director of Libraries for Collection Development, University of Kentucky; James C. Anderson and David Horvath, Photographic Archives, and L. Dale Patterson, University Archives, University of Louisville; and James Wyman and Roger H. D. Rowley, Visual Studies Workshop, Rochester.

Rizzoli's capable staff is responsible for the elegance and legibility of this volume. Jane Fluegel's enthusiasm and love of Meatyard's photography began Rizzoli's involvement with the project; Beth Kugler's and Charles Miers's patient and thorough editing brought the book to its final form. Robert Hennessey's extraordinary ability to reproduce Meatyard's impossibly dark images makes it possible at last to bring a substantial body of excellent reproductions of his work to the public.

At the Akron Art Museum, the entire staff not only assisted with this endeavor either directly or indirectly but also patiently endured my preoccupation with it over a four-year period. My special appreciation goes to staff members Jane Falk, James Williams, Jeffrey Farmer, Ginger Styles, Arlene Rossen, and Lenore Delong-Fiedorek for their extensive assistance in bringing this project to completion. Several volunteers and interns assisted with the research: Julie Novkov, Julianne Duda, Adrienne Miller, and Meredith Palumbo. My personal thanks go not only to those listed above but also to Mitchell Kahan, director of the Akron Art Museum; Christine Havice; and my husband, Mark Soppeland.

Barbara Tannenbaum
Curator, Akron Art Museum

Untitled [Zen Twig; landscape], 1964

Barbara Tannenbaum

Fiction as a Higher Truth: The Photography of Ralph Eugene Meatyard

INTRODUCTION

Only a single copy of Beaumont Newhall's *History of Photography* includes the work of Ralph Eugene Meatyard. In his own copy of the book, Meatyard dry mounted a new frontispiece, his photograph *Romance (N.) From Ambrose Bierce #3*, privately redressing his omission from the text. Newhall's decision not to include Meatyard's work points up the photographer's marginal status in photographic histories written during his lifetime. This position is now being reconsidered from the perspective of the current decade, not only because Meatyard was a brilliant photographer but also because his work investigated and successfully combined several distinct approaches to photography that seem particularly relevant to the art of the late 1980s and the early 1990s.

Meatyard, who gained extensive knowledge of lenses and vision while training as an optician, was obsessed with discovering new ways of seeing particular to the camera, that is, uniquely photographic images. Therefore, he turned to abstraction at times. With such an aim, Meatyard might have produced work that was primarily formalistic, but instead his abstractions are the opposite—dramatic and expressive. The emotional impact of Meatyard's abstractions is derived from a very special impetus, one that informs his figurative work as well. Around 1956, he began learning about the Eastern philosophy and religion, Zen. Believing photography well suited to metaphorical communication, Meatyard used it to convey the spiritual essences that Zen taught him lay behind the visible world. He readily flouted photographic conventions of the time, including sharp focus and a wide range of tonal gradation, in order to achieve these expressive ends. The documentary nature of the medium was also of little consequence to Meatyard: he gladly abandoned the photographer's role as a passive recorder.

Many of his images are fabricated; that is, he posed the models, added props and masks, incorporated multiple exposures, and added other such interventions between found reality and the scene finally recorded on film. Through his art he endeavored to reveal a truth higher than mere fact.

These two interests—the scientific nature of camera vision and the spiritual essence behind the visible world—seem antithetical. Combining them, Meatyard created work that is difficult to place in the context of photographic history. While a strong tradition exists for abstract, expressive, and fictional photography, modern historians have for the most part tried to establish a linear progression based on the camera's ability to record fact. Only recently have they begun to give equal status to the fictional side of the medium. Further complicating interpretation of Meatyard's art is the fact that he drew not only upon the work of historical and contemporary photographers but also upon sources and ideas from different disciplines, including modern painting, contemporary literature, art theory, the philosophy of Zen, and his technical training as an optician. The interdisciplinary origins of his work enrich the photographs but make analyzing them difficult.

Meatyard's status, self-assigned and publicly proclaimed, as a "dedicated amateur" may partly explain his omission from texts such as Newhall's. This status should not be denigrated nor did the artist think of it as second-class citizenship. Instead, he considered it an advantage to be able to pursue his art purely for pleasure. He was well aware of the contributions made to the medium by serious amateurs, beginning with the discovery of the photographic process in the mid-nineteenth century. Meatyard also shared with those early experimenters a background of scientific rather than artistic training. While many artists today support themselves by teaching art, separation of vocation from avocation is not unknown. Just as "Douanier" Rousseau was both customs officer and painter, William Carlos Williams doctor and poet, and Wallace Stevens insurance executive and poet, Ralph Eugene Meatyard was both an optician and a photographer.

By the end of his life, Meatyard was able to connect his two callings to a certain extent. The walls of Eyeglasses of Kentucky, the optical shop he opened in 1967, were hung with an ever-changing exhibition of photographs by professionals such as Emmet Gowin, Bill Burke, Jack Welpott, or Judy Dater, or by students from the Rhode Island School of Design, or even by Ralph Eugene Meatyard himself. On the table in the waiting area, alongside the copies of *Reader's Digest,* were avant-garde literary periodicals to which Meatyard and his friends contributed, such as *The Hudson Review* or *Monk's Pond,* Thomas Merton's magazine published at the monastery of Gethsemani near Bardstown, Kentucky. Also adorning the walls was a photograph of the definition of the word eye from Samuel Johnson's eighteenth-century dictionary. This image was an entirely appropriate emblem for Meatyard, combining references to physical vision, spiritual insight, and literary interests with a self-referential pun thrown in for good measure.[1]

Family was the third major component of his life along with art and career. Devoted to his wife and three children, Meatyard actively pursued family-oriented, all-American activities such as coaching his son's Little League team, serving on the PTA, and organizing family outings. These excursions were frequently turned to the purpose of his photography: family and friends were Meatyard's chief models. Although his works are not autobiographical, they are self-revealing.

THE EDUCATION OF AN ARTIST

Nothing exists; all things are becoming.
—REIHO MASUNAGA[2]

After he graduated from the university high school of Illinois State University in Normal in 1943, Meatyard entered the navy. As part of the V-12 program, he spent one year in a predentistry course of study at Williams College but was transferred to a hospital corps when he became more interested in extracurricular activities such as drama and journalism than in his predentistry classes.[3] When the war ended and Meatyard was discharged, he married and apprenticed as an optician in Chicago. Receiving his license in 1949, Meatyard obtained a job in Bloomington, Illinois, but quit the following year to study philosophy on the GI Bill at Illinois Wesleyan University. After one semester there, he left to accept a job as an optician with Tinder-Krauss-Tinder in Lexington. He continued to work for that firm until he opened his own shop, Eyeglasses of Kentucky, in 1967.

The optical firm where Meatyard worked also sold photographic equipment and supplies. It was there that he purchased his first camera in 1950 in order to photograph his newborn son. However, Meatyard soon progressed from snapshooter to serious amateur photographer. This predilection towards the arts may have come from his family background; it cannot be sheer coincidence that both Meatyard and his younger brother, who is a professor of sculpture and painting, became artists. A number of Meatyard's ancestors and relations were involved with the arts, including a cousin, Thomas Buford Meteyard, who studied in Paris and painted in the impressionist style at Giverny at the turn of the century. Ralph Eugene Meatyard's grandmother was an amateur painter, and his father renovated historic houses for a living.[4]

Meatyard's first education in photography was as a member of the Pictorial Division, or fine art section, of the Photographic Society of America, a national organization composed primarily of amateur photographers. The society regularly held competitions, salons, and exhibitions; Meatyard participated in several of their national shows in 1954 and 1955. Portfolio reviews, in which more experienced photographers judged those with less experience, were available through the mail to members across the country. The P.S.A., which encouraged a photojournalistic approach, prized legibility of narrative and emphasized technique and process. Works by Meatyard from 1954, the year he joined the P.S.A., already contained the seeds of his future use of abstraction, the blurred image, the fabricated or set-up scene, the mask and the doll, and his peculiar sense of dark humor. While these early images lacked the symbolism and poetry, not to mention visual sophistication, of his later work, they were nonetheless unusual enough to make him seem something of an iconoclast to the P.S.A. reviewers.

The Lexington Camera Club, which Meatyard also joined in 1954, was far more accepting of nonconventional and avant-garde work. While it was common in those days for camera clubs to be affiliated with the P.S.A., from its origin the Lexington Camera Club emphasized different values.[5] Rather than subscribing to a single set of principles or advocating one type of work, the Lexington Camera Club felt that each member should choose his own direction. Thus, members used a variety of approaches, from documentary to precisionist to abstract. The club's meetings, an oral corollary to the P.S.A.'s written reviews, consisted of showing and criticizing prints by members and by other photographers.

The club's leader in the early 1950s was Van Deren Coke (see p. 58). He was well qualified, having studied photography in Lexington, at the Clarence White School of Photography in New York, and with Ansel Adams in California, and having met Paul Strand, the Westons, and Alfred Stieglitz.[6] Though Coke was soon to embark on a distinguished career as a photographer, professor of art and art history, and museum curator, in the mid-1950s he was working in Lexington as president of his family's hardware business. He became Meatyard's mentor. In the summer of 1955, Coke held a series of photography classes at his home for the most serious members of the club—including Meatyard—that offered personalized instruction far beyond the scope of the club meetings. Part of the curriculum involved technical matters, such as learning the Zone System, a system of exposure and development codified by Ansel Adams and Minor White, which Meatyard would later adapt for his own purposes. Another lesson Coke taught the group was that exotic locales were not necessary to produce extraordinary images. He encouraged his students to photograph figuratively and literally in their own backyards and followed this practice himself. Meatyard took his advice to heart, photographing exclusively in and around northern Kentucky throughout his career.

The major thrust of Coke's instruction concerned the consideration of the medium as a vehicle for personal expression. He advised his students that not just subject matter but also the formal aspects of a photograph—composition, repetition of forms, use of dark and light, the position of the camera, and the degree of detail—could contribute to a picture's meaning. The group studied original works by the Westons, Stieglitz, Adams, White, Aaron Siskind, and Harry Callahan from Coke's personal collection. Handouts that Coke gave the class included such aphorisms as "our [the photographers'] job in society is revelation" and "the camera sees even beyond the visual consciousness," hinting at an almost shamanistic role for the artist-photographer.[7] Coke's teachings, more than any other factor, encouraged Meatyard to find his own voice.

THE OLD SOUTH #2, c. 1954–1955

While it is difficult to pinpoint the dates of Meatyard's work of the mid-1950s with any certainty, he seems to have developed his thinking about the purposes and uses of photography in 1954–55. A new, more metaphorical style can be seen in *The Old South #2* (p. 17). Composition and tonal values contribute to the meaning of this study in opposites. In the interior of an old, ruined shed, a small boy leans against the frame of an enormous doorway. The shed's foundation has fallen away, leaving the walls askew at a perilous angle. This unstable parallelogram dominates the composition. Meatyard must have found it a successful device, for he returned to it to separate mother and daughter in an untitled work from the early seventies (p. 132). The distribution of darks and lights in *The Old South #2* might have been inherent in the scene's juxtaposition of interior and exterior, but Meatyard exaggerated the contrast. He set his exposure in accordance with the dark interior, thus making details and textures of the shed's walls visible. Intruding into this shadowy, ruined, man-made structure is the light of the natural world. Through the doorway a tree can be seen, young and willowy like the boy beside it. The tree's leaves and the boy's hair dissolve in the purposely overexposed white light, while his dark shirt and legs are silhouetted against it. Nature's potential for growth, associated with light, is juxtaposed with the dark ruin of an aged, human-built structure. The boy, Meatyard's elder son, Michael, is balanced precariously on the threshold between dark and light, belonging in part to each realm. While not as rich as later images, *The Old South #2* contains the seeds of much of Meatyard's later photography: metaphorical use of light and dark, a rigid geometry of composition, and the juxtaposition of youth and nature with civilization's decay.

Despite this emphasis on expressive and creative photography, when Meatyard and Coke, who was a friend as well as mentor, undertook a joint project in 1955–56, it was of a documentary nature. The two men collaborated on a photographic survey of Georgetown Street, a Lexington thoroughfare traveled by Coke as he came into town each day to go to work.[8] The self-imposed task, which the two men approached methodically by compiling a list of addresses and occupants, was to depict a resident, proprietor, or customer of each building in this African-American neighborhood (see pp. 19, 20, 90). The project's antecedents lie in the in-depth documentary projects of the 1930s, including the Farm Security Administration photographs of rural life and the Photo League's documentation of urban squalor. The Photo League, an association of photographers in New York who advocated extensive documentation of urban areas by teams, was committed to using photography to bring about social and political reform. Meatyard and Coke did not share these aims. On the contrary, they set out to present what Meatyard termed "an impersonal view."[9] Coke said the inspiration for the Georgetown project came from the desire to photograph various motifs found on the street. Notably, it was in this same year, 1955, that Robert Frank began his editorial photographic odyssey through the United States. Perhaps because Meatyard lacked the reforming zeal and passion of the 1930s groups or the critical eye of Frank, the Georgetown images are, for the most part, unremarkable.

While individual images may be weak, the series was important to Meatyard's development as a photographer. It constitutes his most extensive group of portraits, serving as a precursor to the smaller series of portraits of literary figures he would undertake in the late 1960s and to the later Lucybelle Crater series. Meatyard could be an excellent portraitist, as can be seen in the stark bust-length

UNTITLED [Georgetown series: woman entering store], c. 1955–56

shot of a man with a cigarette (p. 20). Also, it was during this period that he began experimenting effectively with the blurred figure and with the expressive use of light. In the image of four children playing marbles (p. 90), these formal devices draw the viewer's attention to an unknown and mysterious element outside the picture frame. This sense of a presence and space existing beyond the visible area is a characteristic of many Meatyard photographs. It engages viewers, asking them to use their imagination to supply their own solution to the mystery. The Georgetown series may also have been Meatyard's first experience of working in a series, a practice he would continue throughout his lifetime.

UNTITLED [Georgetown series: portrait of man with hat], 1956

Meatyard undertook a second documentary series by himself during that same period, a visual catalogue of tombstones in a Lexington cemetery (see p. 21). These images, which are primarily informational, led to a later, more metaphorical series of funerary statuary (pp. 94–95).

The summer following Coke's class, Meatyard and his teacher attended a workshop at Indiana University. Many of the workshop's concepts had already been introduced to Meatyard by Coke, who was certainly familiar with the work and theories of instructors Henry Holmes Smith, Aaron Siskind, and Minor White, but the workshop codified and reinforced those ideas. The validity of photography as a fine art of equivalent stature to painting or sculpture was stressed by all three teachers. Siskind, who taught at the Institute of Design in Chicago (the descendant of Laszlo Moholy-Nagy's New Bauhaus[10]), discussed the importance of photographers' studying other media as well as other art forms to enrich their work. He led the group on shooting expeditions and suggested, along with White, the exploration of inanimate materials such as rocks as vehicles for the expression of universal human experience.

The majority of the three weeks was spent not in shooting pictures but rather in practicing "picture reading," a form of visual and iconographic analysis based on literary and art historical methodologies. Smith, who organized the workshop, adapted his terms and techniques of analysis from literary criticism, especially the writings of I. A. Richards.[11] An important advocate and practitioner

UNTITLED [Gravestone: Samuel F. Cassell], 1955

of abstract photography and technical experimentation, Smith was a direct link with the theories of design and expression espoused by the Bauhaus; he was instrumental in setting up the New Bauhaus in Chicago in 1937. In addition to analysis of finished photographs, Smith discussed two opposing methods of picture taking and possibilities for their combination: one approach relied on intuition and accident; the other, often termed previsualization, insisted upon control.

For those workshop participants choosing the former approach, Minor White presented a seven-part discipline for intuition—a technique to improve and structure one's awareness. White, who presided over the majority of the sessions, drew upon stylistic, iconographic, and formal analysis for his discussions of photography. He presented a seven-part method—derived from art historian Heinrich Wöfflin's *Principles of Art History* (1915)—that considered lighting, planemetric versus recessional space, closed versus open structure, literal versus metaphorical images, and the portrayal of time as the major principles of photography. White also differentiated among levels of meaning (based loosely on art historian Erwin Panofsky's levels of iconography and iconology), from a simple emblem to a sign to a complex symbol.[12] During the workshop, White recommended a number of books he considered crucial to the education of a photographer. Among these were two books on Zen that started Meatyard on his exploration of that philosophy.

Untitled [Photograph of abstract painting on glass], c. 1957–58

Meatyard strongly advocated the principles he had learned in Indiana. Immediately upon his return from the summer workshop, he taught a series of seminars based on them for some members of the Lexington Camera Club.[13] In seminars conducted in later years, Meatyard continued to address these same topics and issues, especially consciousness of formal structure and its relationship to meaning, and the combination of intuition and previsualization.[14]

The years following the Indiana workshop represented a concentrated period of self-directed intellectual and visual exploration for Meatyard. An energetic, strong-minded, and committed individual, he set himself tasks of no small ilk: an examination of the relationship between painting and photography (which may have been inspired by Siskind's comments) and an extensive set of readings on art theory. Because of his full-time job as an optician, these projects and his photography had to be pursued in the evenings and on weekends.

In order to explore the boundaries between painting and photography, Meatyard decided to execute paintings exclusively for the purpose of photographing them in black and white. A diary Meatyard kept in December 1957 and through the winter of 1958 chronicles his ventures as a painter, which he continued into 1959.[15] Producing not just the photograph but also the thing to be photographed permitted a symbolic removal from the reality usually held to be a fundamental characteristic of photography. At the same time, it allowed for manipulation of and total control over all elements. The majority of his paintings were abstract. Some consisted of geometric shapes painted on sandwiched sheets of glass, using the support's transparency as a formal element (p. 22).[16]

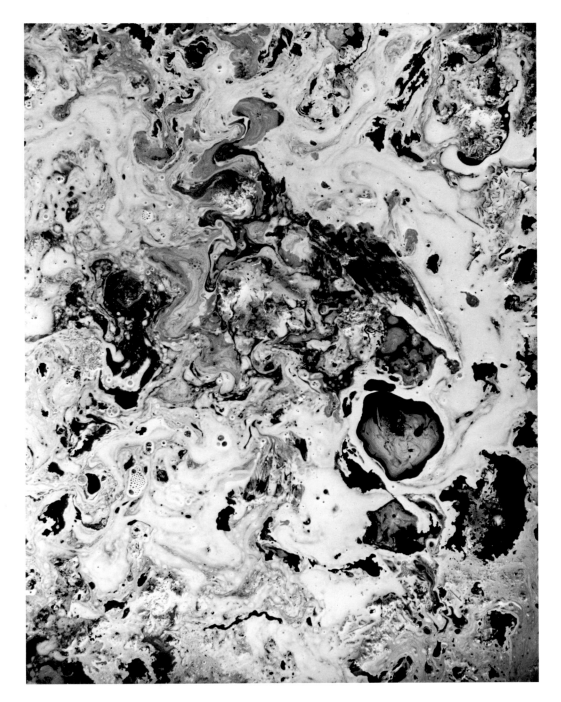

ICE [Bird in paint and ice], c. 1957–58

Other, more ephemeral paintings, called "paintings in ice" by the artist, incorporated a degree of chance into their production. Paints and other items—including birds' carcasses—were added to freezing water contained in large developing trays placed outdoors. When the water had just frozen or was barely in motion due to wind or slight agitation, Meatyard took the photograph. He controlled the format, the colors, and the items to be included, but he left the final composition to chance and the forces of nature. Meatyard eliminated the edges of the tray from the photograph, letting the materials fill the frame and creating an all-over composition not unlike abstract expressionist paintings of the time.

Meatyard began another series visually related to abstract expressionism in 1957: he photographed the abstract patterning found in the textures of natural or man-made surfaces. He continued making these close-up, "straight" shots of found surfaces, including rocks, ice, mud, walls, and glass (pp. 97, 98, 99), into 1960. The concept and subject matter were probably inspired by similar work by Minor White, Harry Callahan, and Aaron Siskind. However, the images resemble abstract expressionist paintings more than their photographic antecedents. Some of Meatyard's prints recall the broad gestural strokes of Franz Kline, others the delicate hatchings of Morris Graves (whom he mentioned several times in his diary). In notes describing some of his photographs, Meatyard used faces, figures, and religious symbolism to describe apparently abstract compositions. However, in later discussions of these early works, he referred to them as totally abstract. In the 1958 diary, Meatyard discussed abstraction as a path to universal imagery. "The more universal anything is the more abstract it must be," he wrote.[17] One artist who interested him was the Swiss painter Paul Klee, whose *Pedagogical Sketchbook* (1925) Meatyard owned. Like Klee, Meatyard demanded that his abstractions convey feelings, moods, and emotions. And, like the painter, Meatyard systematically explored (and taught) possible systems of emotional equivalents for formal elements such as composition, tonality, and shape.

Although Meatyard lived far from the center of the art world and rarely traveled, he was nonetheless well versed in modern and contemporary art, photography, and literature through his readings and through communications with other photographers. His library, which numbered over eighteen hundred volumes by the time of his death, covered a wide range of topics to suit his eclectic tastes. He read constantly and seriously but eccentrically—out of choice, not duty. Meatyard studied his books assiduously, writing private commentary on their contents, taking extensive reading notes, or annotating passages.

In addition to numerous art books and periodicals dealing with modern art—especially surrealism—and with art theory, Meatyard had an extensive collection of writings on photography.[18] These included a nearly full run of *Aperture* magazine—even the early issues, which date from before his own involvement with the medium; several issues of Alfred Stieglitz's magazine, *Camera Work;* esoteric publications such as single issues of photography magazines and yearbooks from around the world; and more common, commercial magazines, such as *Popular Photography* and *U.S. Camera.*

PAGES FROM MEATYARD'S NOTEBOOK OF ODD NAMES

    The largest single category of books in Meatyard's library was not visual arts or photography but rather literature, including poetry, fiction, literary criticism, and history. He read literature out of personal interest but also out of friendship. Beginning in 1960, when the poet, photographer, and publisher Jonathan Williams was passing through Lexington and looked him up, Meatyard became friends with a number of literary figures, including poet, painter, and scholar Guy Davenport; poet and environmental essayist Wendell Berry; poet, monk, and Christian theologian Thomas Merton; photographer, poet, and publisher Jonathan Greene; and poet and photographer James Baker Hall. Through these friends, he made the acquaintance of avant-garde filmmaker Stan Brakhage, poet Denise Levertov, critic Parker Tyler, poet Louis Zukofsky, and literary historian and critic Hugh Kenner, among others. Time spent with them was not only pleasurable but also educational, exposing Meatyard to many sources and ideas that might not otherwise have captured his attention.

    Though a quiet man, Meatyard was a great companion—"affable, congenial, wonderful sense of humor," according to Davenport.[19] Artists themselves, his friends appreciated the opportunity to see the world through his unique vision. "The most important thing to know about Gene," said Davenport, "is that he adored the outrageous. . . . He had many passions . . . [such as] his collection of [do] 'you believe it?' recordings—the Andrews Sisters singing the Raven of Poe . . . [and] the wedding of Sister Rosetta Tharpe. . . . He collected peculiar names and he loved peculiar facts, too, such as the fact that in Kentucky you can actually get a driver's license if you're legally but not totally blind."[20] Meatyard also had a fabulous collection of early jazz recordings, which were not only listed by title but also cross-indexed by song and artist. The odd names he collected were sorted and neatly penned in a notebook (p. 25) with the intent of eventual publication. Meatyard's approach to these varied and wonderfully eccentric hobbies was as purposeful and intense as his practice of photography. Meatyard's was, perhaps, the best kind of education—one undertaken purely out of curiosity and a love of knowledge, art, and literature.

Although Meatyard's education was a continuing one, the time came when the delicate threshold between student and independent artist was crossed. During the mid-1950s, he developed his individual style and characteristic subject matter, but not until the last years of that decade did his work attain a consistently high quality and purposeful direction. In terms of local authority, his change in status was confirmed around 1956 when his mentor departed, making Meatyard the dominant figure in the Lexington Camera Club: the pupil became the teacher. Meatyard enjoyed this status but was not satisfied by it; he wanted very much to make a significant contribution to the field of photography. His ambition, evident in his 1958 diary and his artist's statements from the late 1950s and early 1960s, was directed toward finding a new way of seeing rather than achieving commercial success (which was practically nonexistent for fine art photographers at that time anyway). This quest allowed him to combine his optician's knowledge of lenses and the eye with the issues of aesthetics and appropriate content raised by his photographic training. In 1957 Meatyard began the first of several series concerned with perception as experienced by the camera rather than the human eye.

LIGHT ON WATER

It is only shallow people who do not judge by appearances. The mystery of the world is in the visible, not the invisible.

—OSCAR WILDE

Every year from 1957 until his death in 1972, Meatyard made a group of photos of direct sunlight reflected on the surface of a pond or river. Capturing the marriage of opposites so typical of Meatyard's work, the Light on Water series (most often referred to by the artist as his "light" or "lite" pictures) can be seen as pictures of fire dancing on water.[21] The earliest ones can be read literally as well as abstractly. Despite soft focus, ripples of wind on the water and light on the leaves can be seen in *Untitled* (Light on Water), from 1957–58 (p. 107).

By 1959 the images quickly move away from any literal reading to become magical dramas of light streaking across fields of darkness (pp. 108, 109, 111). In *Light #3* (Light on Water) of 1959 (p. 27), described in one of the artist's

LIGHT #3 [Light on Water], 1959

notebooks as "burning water," flames of light shoot up from the water's surface, drawn by some invisible source toward the upper-left corner of the picture. Meatyard presents an astounding, Dante-like inferno, seductive nonetheless in its visual beauty. Some of the Light on Water images are more lyrical in their abstraction. Others encourage the viewer to read in figurative content, such as plants (p. 109), human faces, or symbols (p. 112). This is the same kind of visual dreaming that leads one to find an animal figure "hidden" in a cloud's form or, as in Alfred Stieglitz's Equivalents series, to equate abstract cloud forms with emotions.[22]

Although complex compositionally, the prints appear to be technically straightforward studies of light and darkness. This straightforwardness is an illusion. According to Meatyard's notebooks, at least some of the images are printed in the negative; that is, he exchanged lights for darks. Such a practice was exceedingly rare for Meatyard; this may be its only occurrence.[23] The Light on Water negatives are dense, which was also unusual for Meatyard, and they often have more light areas than show up on the final prints. By lengthening the exposure during printing, Meatyard could limit the tonalities to bright lights and heavy darks and greatly reduce areas of middle tone.[24]

In addition to extreme contrasts, time and motion also entered into the making of these pictures. Though the camera was hand-held, exposures were of long duration, occasionally lasting whole seconds. Meatyard sometimes used multiple exposures, moving the camera so that areas he knew were dark would receive bits of light on them. Or he might move the camera rhythmically along the path of the moving water. Most often, he pointed the camera straight at the water, with the focal plane of the camera parallel to the water's surface. However, because of the compositions and directional quality to the markings, the viewer senses not a flat space without gravity but a three-dimensional world with depth.

There are a number of photographic antecedents for exploring light as abstract form, including Francis Bruguière's light abstractions using cut paper of the 1920s, Lotte Jacobi's photogenics of the 1940s and 1950s, Carlotta Corpron's light graphics, and Frederick Sommer's experiments. Gyorgy Kepes and other faculty at the Institute of Design in Chicago encouraged the exploration of experimental and abstract photography.[25] Light as a spiritual force was also an important element in the work of Minor White. Closest to Meatyard's work, however, are Harry Callahan's pictures of sunlight on water, done in 1943, which Meatyard may have seen at the Indiana workshop, through Coke, or in reproduction.[26] Though they are photographs of the same subject, Meatyard's images differ from Callahan's in spirit. Callahan's are primarily abstract studies; they are almost lyrical, emphasizing line and pattern over emotion.[27] Meatyard's, by contrast, are very much about expressive content; drama, texture, and gesture are dominant.

The physical translation of motion and emotion found in abstract expressionist painting is closely related in spirit to Meatyard's Light on Water images. He talked about creating the work as "drawing and constructing an abstracted picture all of my own."[28] Meatyard was familiar with the paintings of the abstract expressionists through reproductions in art books and magazines. The light on the moving water becomes, in Meatyard's post-1958 works, a stroke capturing energy in motion. Sometimes these gestures were built up by exposure to form a purely visual texture, a highly energized surface reminiscent of the skeins of paint in the work of Jackson Pollock (see *Notes On The Keyboard Of The Imagination—#1*, 1962; p. 109). Meatyard's images also call to mind the "white writings"—gestural markings of white paint that resemble script—in the paintings of Mark Tobey and Morris Graves, artists to whom Meatyard referred in his diary. They shared with him a strong interest in Zen, an appreciation of the calligraphic strokes of Far Eastern art, and a mystical attitude toward the relationship between art and nature.

It is possible to consider Meatyard's "strokes" in terms of aural as well as optical analogies. His images usually have a strong rhythm, with repetitions, syncopations, and pauses. These visual rhythms are reminiscent of the aural rhythms of the early-twentieth-century jazz music he greatly enjoyed.[29] The intuition and chance occurrence involved in the making of his "light" pictures is akin to jazz improvisation: a response to the circumstance and mood, a structured freedom.

For Meatyard, such freedom was circumscribed by certain rules. He publicly declared his adherence "to the techniques of the earliest and most sincere workers of the camera—straight, unmanipulated pictures. That which I present is that which I see. However, I work a great deal in romantic-surrealist as well as abstract for I feel that 'more real than real' is the special province of the serious photographer."[30] With few exceptions, Meatyard adhered to this principle—in the darkroom. Manipulations done in the darkroom that were not part of the normal developing and printing process, such as cropping and a normal amount of dodging and burning, were untruthful and strictly avoided. Meatyard stayed close to the image in the negative. However, almost any manipulation done up to and including the moment of the actual exposure was acceptable to him: fabricating and posing the scene, staging movement by photographer or model during an exposure, holding his hand over the lens to add mysterious shadows, and other such interventions into found reality. He did not merely photograph what was in front of his camera, he arranged for the camera to see certain things. The point was to achieve not documentary faithfulness but an abstract or symbolic representation that came closer to a higher reality.

Light, the subject matter in this series, served Meatyard not just as an avenue for exploring abstract form, gesture, and rhythm, but also as a way to represent spiritual energy—the light within. Meatyard said that "light alone [is] the subject of the photographs. One source, many sources—direct, reflected. Coming from within. Wherever light, is heavenly light."[31] Light is not just an essential characteristic of photography: it is at the core of human existence. Vision is possible because of it; our world could not exist without its life-giving energy. Perhaps because of its biological importance, light has also come to represent spiritual and intellectual illumination. For Meatyard, abstraction was a means, not an end. "I have never made an abstracted photograph without content," he wrote.[32]

In earlier times, artists liked to show what was actually
visible, either the things they liked to look at or things they would like
to have seen. Nowadays, we are concerned with reality
rather than with the merely visible.

—PAUL KLEE

In 1958 Meatyard began a second series of work concerned with discovering new kinds of photographic vision, the No-Focus images. In that year, Meatyard began re-examining his previous photographs and found them lacking. This retrospective period coincided with his series of photographs of abstracted textural surfaces and his attempts at painting. It may have been a heightened awareness of this latter medium that led him to look at the work of local artists. Seeing the hard-edged abstract paintings of Frederic Thursz, a University of Kentucky faculty member, Meatyard worried that hard-edged abstraction spelled "the *end* of the growth in photograph[y]."[33] He found Thursz's paintings, while abstract, to be extremely photographic in their concern with and handling of lines, shapes, and edges. Meatyard felt that the painter had far greater control over these qualities than the photographer. If painting could replicate or perhaps even exceed the expressive qualities currently thought of as photographic, of what use was fine art photography?

Meatyard wanted his work to respond to questions prevalent in art criticism at the time about the strength and validity of photography as an art medium. Some critics attacked photography as an inherently weak medium because its subjects were always recognizable and thus it was incapable of producing pure expression unrelated to the physical world. Others claimed that anyone standing in the same spot would take the same photograph, that the art of photography was in the finding rather than the making.[34] Meatyard decided to seek out new characteristics of vision that were unique to the camera's lens, "new aspects of art belonging only to photography."[35]

Months of intense deliberation passed as Meatyard tried to solve this problem.[36] Surveying his past work, Meatyard began to be attracted to the out-of-focus backgrounds in some of the images. One of Van Deren Coke's precepts for making a photograph was finding an appropriate background, then putting something in front of it. Meatyard followed this practice in making his pictures. Thus his backgrounds were carefully selected and the finished images carefully previsualized.[37] He decided to elevate these backgrounds to the status of primary subject matter. Instead of producing out-of-focus pictures with recognizable images, which he felt had already been done, Meatyard would make pictures with no focus at all. Edges would consist of bringing two tone masses together, thus ridding photography—at least in the instance of these pictures—of what Meatyard called "its most distasteful . . . characteristic: that of sharpness, of planes so close together that line was imposed without meaning to do it."[38] As was true of much of his work, Meatyard felt he should be able to control all the formal elements of the picture. What he might find to shoot could be left somewhat up to chance and intuition, but how the photograph was made—its exposure, composition, and symbolic content—should be consciously and purposefully constructed.

Achieving successful No-Focus photographs was far more difficult than coming up with the idea. At first, Meatyard tried choosing a subject, throwing the lens out of focus, and then shooting it. This did not work. "I found that I had to learn to see No-Focus from the beginning," he wrote.[39] He spent three months walking around looking through an unfocused camera before he felt ready to capture an image on film. Though the lens might be out of focus, the other elements of photography, from exposure to printing, nonetheless had to be clean, clear, and sharp to produce a good image.[40] The No-Focus images were harder to shoot than his other work. Meatyard was in the habit of shooting four or five rolls a day when he was photographing, but he was only able to take one to one and a half rolls a day of the No-Focus pictures. He would then wait two to three months before developing them.[41] After that interval, he was no longer able to identify the scenes or objects by looking at the works; he had succeeded, at least for himself, in detaching the images from the bit of reality on which they had been based.

The No-Focus pictures (pp. 100–105) float between abstraction and reality. All of them impart a sense of objects in a larger world, but some (pp. 101, 102, 104) lack referents, becoming forms of pure light set in darkness. Other No-Focus works, ones with grays as well as blacks and whites (p. 103), resemble X rays, as if the camera were looking through rather than at a form. In the most abstract ones, there are no clear boundaries between forms and the spaces next to them. Thus, there can be no foreground or background. Although a certain amount of depth results from lights coming forward and darks receding, the entire picture area is of equal importance.

After a hiatus in late 1959 and early 1960, Meatyard returned in the spring of 1960 to No-Focus, producing works with readable figures (p. 105) that seem to maintain a stronger connection with the identifiable world. This connection, however, may be illusory. Meatyard said these later pictures were "abstracted pictures of people or things that were people or things [that] look like people or things."[42] Characteristically, he did not identify which were which, nor did he want that to be clear to the viewer. These later, more figurative images resemble Harry Callahan's exploration of focus around 1953, which Meatyard may very well have seen.[43] The two sets of images share high contrast and an almost total elimination of detail, but Callahan's photographs are out of focus, as opposed to No-Focus. The gender, build, and pose of Callahan's figures are readily identifiable, while Meatyard's are far more abstracted and distorted.

The eye wants to bring the No-Focus images into focus yet is stymied. Nothing is immediately recognizable and yet everything seems somehow familiar. The result, though frustrating at times, is the active involvement of the viewer's eye and imagination in the act of looking. Meatyard described the ambiguity these images create as "a coming and going, a glance, the touch of a hand, a growing and a dissolving—whispers and shouts."[44] Although he stopped producing No-Focus images in 1960, Meatyard looked back on them in 1969 and wrote descriptions of several.[45] His own response to *No-Focus #3* (p. 100) was "white is the least of us, dark is the most; spirit of the black bird as seen by the spirit of me; return and face the seen; dance of mostly consequential things."[46] His words are like haiku in their evocative allusions and comparisons, but they avoid identifying any specific subject matter.

Differing interpretations of these and other photographs were quite acceptable to Meatyard. Although he enjoyed showing his art to friends and colleagues, he never interpreted it for them. When he did discuss his pictures, he tended to restrict his comments to formal issues rather than to explicate content or expressive purpose. He certainly believed that it was possible to give a work of art an incorrect reading, but he rarely contradicted others' readings of his work.[47] This desire to let the pictures breathe, to endow them with a sense of becoming rather than of resolution, is a quality that Meatyard would continue to expand in other types of work, particularly his later figurative photographs involving masks and blurred images.

In an essay Meatyard wrote in about 1961 on No-Focus, he expressed a desire to expand No-Focus to incorporate time and motion.[48] Those goals, however, were not accomplished in the No-Focus images but in the later Motion-Sound pictures and the figurative narratives with blurred images. By the time he wrote that essay, Meatyard had already moved away from No-Focus. He did not totally abandon that way of working but instead incorporated it into a new series of pictures, the Zen Twigs.

ZEN TWIGS

Art is the conscious apprehension of the unconscious ecstasy
of all created things.

—CYRIL CONNOLLY

It was Meatyard's son Christopher who applied the term Zen Twigs to this series because the photographs resemble Zen calligraphic drawings—studies that capture nature's movement and energy in simple, linear, gestural strokes.[49] According to the artist's own estimation, about 90 percent of the picture area of these photographs is No-Focus; the remaining 10 percent consists of a sharply focused section of twig, branch, or leaf.[50] The area in focus, the focal plane, is small, concentrating on a single detail.[51] Because that detail is part of a larger whole, our eye is inevitably and rather rapidly drawn into the No-Focus background, a dynamic pattern of lights and darks, lines, and tone forms. In some of the im-

UNTITLED [Zen Twig], 1961

ages, this use of selective focus is complemented with the use of a blur suggesting slight motion, either of the twig or the camera.

Meatyard produced the Zen Twig photographs from approximately 1958 to 1965.[52] Examples were published almost immediately in Van Deren Coke's 1959 *Aperture* article on the artist. In the text, Coke described them as "tone patterns resembling X ray pictures of the human form."[53] Though there are a few images with all-over patterns, most of the twigs bear a resemblance to stick figures fleshed out by the gray tones surrounding them or to ideographic representations of the human body in motion (see pp. 33, 115). In addition to their relationship to Far Eastern calligraphic drawings, the twigs' graceful, gestural forms call to mind abstract expressionist paintings, including the "white writings" of Mark Tobey and Morris Graves, Charles Burchfield's energetically twisted versions of flora,[54] and, of course, Meatyard's own Light on Water series.

In the Zen Twigs and Light on Water series, Meatyard collaborated with nature to produce the strokes. Unlike the No-Focus works, it is important that the viewer identify the subjects of the Zen Twigs as natural forms. Meatyard employed a visual device akin to the literary one of synecdoche, in which one part stands for the whole and the particular represents the general. The relatively minute focused area becomes a symbol of the whole tree and of the life force flowing through it. The visual energy of the dancing lines of the twigs expresses in microcosm the potential for growth and movement in seemingly static objects. Van Deren Coke has suggested that Meatyard's use of these simple natural objects to say something about larger aspects of life resembles Stieglitz's Equivalents; both series affirm the oneness of all natural forms.[55]

Meatyard's empathy for nature and his sense of the fluid boundaries between objects and the spiritual and natural energy inherent in them derived in large part from his interest in Zen. For example, Meatyard discussed his absorption in the place and the moment: "To be able to feel on your back the dew as it lies on a blade of grass; to be able to feel ice at the instant it turns to water; . . . when you eat, when you sleep . . . this is Zen."[56] The narrowly restricted field of focus of the twigs becomes a Zen exercise. The finished pictures, like most Meatyard prints, are small in scale and intimate in feel. Drawing the viewer in, the picture inspires meditation on a single countenance of nature, at the same time making it clear that the minute fragment holds a significance much larger than its size.

Zen became an important influence on Meatyard's work and life beginning in the mid-1950s. "Zen and I came together when introduced to two books . . . recommended for photography by Minor [White]," wrote Meatyard in a 1960 letter to Van Deren Coke. "It is a philosophy more than religion and a thing to do more than to talk about."[57] At the time of his death, his library contained thirty-three books on Far Eastern religions, including many of the classic works on Zen, which were well-annotated by the artist. Meatyard seems to have carried on these studies in isolation, without contact with instructors, spiritual leaders, or other followers. He found Zen a helpful guide for daily life and felt free to adapt it to fulfill his own needs and those of others.[58] In the early 1960s, Meatyard used Zen to counsel and comfort his friend and fellow member of the Lexington Camera Club Cranston Ritchie during Ritchie's protracted and eventually fatal battle with cancer. Meatyard also saw Zen as an aesthetic force. Seconding Minor White's interest in Zen as particularly applicable to photography, Meatyard found its principles in much photography he admired, including the work of Edward Weston, Alfred Stieglitz, Paul Strand, and Van Deren Coke.[59] Meatyard enjoyed its influence on literature as well, reading the works of poets and writers such as Jack Kerouac, Henry Miller, Allen Ginsberg, Gary Snyder, Charles Olson, and Louis Zukofsky.

It was not until January 1967, when he made the acquaintance of monk, author, teacher, photographer, and religious philosopher Thomas Merton, that Meatyard knew someone who was equally or even more knowledgeable on the subject of Zen. Also self-taught in Zen, Merton wrote several books that proposed a complementary relationship for Zen and Christianity. With common interests in literature and photography as well as Zen, the two exchanged postcards, images, and numerous visits (including Rabelaisian picnics at Gethsemani, the Trappist monastery in Kentucky where Merton lived and taught) until the monk's accidental death in late 1968. Merton sent his manuscripts and books to Meatyard for comments and suggestions. Meatyard took portraits of Merton (p. 75) and gave him photographs to use in his books and in *Monk's Pond*, the magazine Merton published briefly.[60]

Meatyard began designating photos as "Zen" or "Z" on the back of the prints and in his notebooks in 1959. He applied this designation to many types of work, not just the twigs, and in 1961, he stated that "an educated background of Zen influences all my photographs."[61] His earlier attempts to find a uniquely photographic way of seeing, such as No-Focus, were subsumed in this new quest. Meatyard now sought vision—an understanding based on the fluid links between the physical, the visual, and the spiritual—rather than mere sight. "Zen," he said, "binds things together, or rather separates them into a single thing."[62]

MOTION-SOUND

Everything going on at once proves agreeable to the
intelligent eye.

—RALPH EUGENE MEATYARD

Meatyard's final series emphasizing unique possibilities for camera vision were the Motion-Sound pictures—complex images in which multiple exposure is the primary visual characteristic. In this body of work, produced between 1967 and 1972, Meatyard was able to accomplish an earlier goal projected for No-Focus: to "represent in the area of a single picture, the equivalent of several frames of a motion picture, or several actions of life . . . to express the movement and the passing of a time that is relative to me, to my life."[63]

Meatyard first experimented with multiple exposure around 1955, but he did not begin to employ the technique in depth until his Light on Water series, begun in 1957. Ironically, multiple exposure is not readily apparent in those images. It was not until 1964–66 that Meatyard once again explored its possibilities as a primary visual motif, superimposing two locales. Like the earliest multiple exposures, these efforts were not entirely successful. Meatyard did not arrive at the Motion-Sound pictures until 1967.

The Motion-Sound pictures resemble a printed image that has been run just a little bit out of register for several impressions. Meatyard told some friends that he kicked the tripod in order to make these images. They do look as if that might have been the case.[64] Despite this touch of humor, Meatyard in fact held the camera by hand, taking one base exposure, then shifting or rotating the camera slightly on an axis running through the plane of the lens and exposing the negative again. The camera's motion might be circular (see p. 164), vertical as in the first image in *The Unforeseen Wilderness* series (p. 172), horizontal as in *16—#8 Motion* (p. 166), or diagonal as in *19–#11 Motion* (p. 171). This procedure was repeated; some of the Motion-Sound pictures have as many as three exposures. The viewer is actively involved in these photographs in the same way as in the No-Focus work. Effort and concentration are required to identify the scene and bring it into focus, yet that is not always possible.

Most of the images show natural settings, perhaps because Meatyard was simultaneously working on a series of photographs of Kentucky's Red River Gorge. Motion-Sound can make the forest look hostile, as in *Untitled* (Motion-Sound: forest; p. 165). Trunks, bare wintery branches, and their shadows, multiplied many times by motion, become impediments to entry. This is animism taken to an extreme, the energy vibration of the microcosmic Zen Twigs heard at its full, almost deafening volume. Like the Zen Twigs, these photographs materialize the force and potency of nature.

Meatyard produced a number of Motion-Sound works showing architecture (pp. 168–170), usually in decay or under demolition. Because of the regular geometry and normal stability of man-made structures, these vibrating buildings may be more disturbing than the images of nature. However, *Untitled* (Motion-Sound: building/mask; p. 168) contains elements of humor as well as sadness. Through composition and framing, Meatyard turned the wall of a building in the process of being torn down into a simplified, geometric mask. It is, of course, one of the functions of a wall to mask activity from the outside. A central strip of wall becomes a nose and two windows become eyes. Through these windows (or reflected in them, it is not clear) can be seen parts of other buildings. The vibration here is very slight, frustrating the eye's natural desire to focus or to distinguish the separate exposures. This tremor signals the fragility of human accomplishments: even the most solid walls eventually come tumbling down. A small, desolate bush at the bottom center, forming a mouth, introduces a touch of nature into the city, but it seems as endangered as the remnants of this building.

Humans, on their rare appearance in this series, are equally imperiled. They are small figures in a swaying landscape or, as in the photograph of Wendell Berry (p. 171), have fallen victim to a greater power. Photographed from above at an extreme angle, Berry's body seems to be disintegrating; his head has already disappeared into the inhospitable rocks that cover the ground. Berry was actually laughing when the photograph was taken, but instead he appears as a dead man caught in the process of abandoning the materiality of the body.[65] Here as in many other of his photographs, Meatyard detaches himself from reality. The camera abandons its pretensions to documentation and readily assumes a fictional stance that underlines the ambiguity of visual "truth."

There are strong ties between the Motion-Sound photographs and other art forms. Motion pictures come to mind immediately. Meatyard also described the Motion-Sound images as musical compositions: "It was this quivering that was coming from them to you setting up a vibration. . . . I orchestrate them and I make symphonies out of them."[66] Meatyard hoped to take photography to yet another realm, one that went beyond its normal visual capabilities. The title he gave this series indicates his ambition: to endow still photography with the ability to express sound and movement.[67] While he may not have achieved a total mixing of the senses, Meatyard did incorporate time and motion into still photography, using them successfully for expressive as well as formal ends.

In addition to music, there are analogies in the Motion-Sound photographs to modernist painting. Meatyard's fragmented picture plane recalls the broken-up planes and simultaneous multiple views of reality in the paintings of Paul Cézanne and the cubists. Meatyard was well acquainted with their work through the books in his library as well as through discussions with friends.[68] Some of the Motion-Sound compositions, while never totally abandoning their relationship to the physical world, become almost abstract. In *Untitled* (Motion-Sound: abstracted tree; p. 167) leaves form a bright, intricate swirl around a tree trunk and branches blackened by heightened contrast. The skeins of dark laid across the bright white light create a dense, chaotic visual field reminiscent of the paint skeins layered by abstract expressionist Jackson Pollock. The identities of tree and leaf become visually subordinated to the struggle between light and dark, between energy and solid matter. Not only are these works multiple exposures, they are also open to multiple readings. Though the Motion-Sound images grew out of a technical process, they move beyond vision to insight, beyond technique to metaphor. Meatyard, though frequently occupied with seeking out new aspects of camera vision, immediately turned those formal devices to expressive ends.

THE UNFORESEEN WILDERNESS:
THE RED RIVER GORGE

The perception of beauty is a moral test.

—HENRY DAVID THOREAU

The equation of morality and beauty is illustrated in Meatyard's photographs of the Red River Gorge, a wilderness area in Kentucky (pp. 82, 172–175). In 1967, when the U.S. Corps of Engineers made plans to flood the entire area by building a dam, Wendell Berry invited Meatyard to collaborate on a book that would convey the gorge's essence and importance. Berry's essay and Meatyard's photographs, published together in 1971 in a book called *The Unforeseen Wilderness,* were an eloquent plea to save the gorge. For three and a half years, Meatyard explored and photographed the area, traveling on foot and by canoe. Sometimes he and Berry traveled together, but most of the time they worked alone, coming together periodically to exchange the fruits of their independent labors. And their labors were fruitful: parts of the gorge were preserved and remain wilderness today.

Though they argue for the preservation of nature, Meatyard's photographs are not soothing pictures of an idyllic landscape. They are as tough as sheer rock and as complex as the rest of his work. In his essay, Berry introduces the character of the photographer—a seer rather than a looker, one who goes to a place "for the real news of it."

> [His] pictures . . . are not ornaments or relics, but windows and doors, enlargements of our living spaces, entrances into the mysterious world outside the walls, lessons in what to look for and how to see. . . . They make us a little afraid, for they suggest always the presence of the unknown, what lies outside the picture and beyond eyesight; they suggest the possibility of the sudden accesses of delight, vision, beauty, joy that entice us to keep alive and reward us for the living; they can serve as spiritual landmarks in the pilgrimage to the earth that each one of us must undertake alone.[69]

A Motion-Sound image of a path was actually the first photograph in the series (p. 172), though it was edited out prior to publication. This shuddering vibration starts the hiker on his or her journey. The multiple exposure suggests both the motion of the hiker and the "unconscious, invisible ecstasy of all created things."[70] Meatyard described these pictures as showing "what is not always seen."[71] The rest of the photographs give no intimation of human presence besides the eye of the camera/photographer.

The Red River Gorge prints are harsh, with strong contrasts between light and dark. They are visceral pictures: a tangle of bare branches becomes a system of veins and bodily organs (p. 174).[72] Shadows are foreboding as sunlight burns its way through the trees to warm the valleys and crevices. Fog glistening on a dark river (p. 82) seems to flow out of a mysterious, narrow passage hidden by foliage, almost as if what is "beyond eyesight" were the source of all water and light, perhaps the source of creation itself.

There are few vistas in the Red River Gorge series; most of the shots are of fairly shallow spaces. The pictures are square or slightly vertical, which is a break from the conventional horizontal format for landscape, and the compositions tend to emphasize flatness and abstraction. These characteristics, along with the high contrast, keep the images on the surface of the print, formally emphasizing the landscape's inaccessibility.

The journey Meatyard and Berry ask us to make is not a physical one. *The Unforeseen Wilderness* is about man's moral relationship to the forces of nature, which can nourish and sustain but can also destroy. The text enumerates man's failings in this relationship and the grim destiny such behavior prophesies. Meatyard's photographs concentrate on nature, presenting both its faces—light and darkness, beauty and awesome force. Man can try to understand the land as he walks through it, but there are always blocked vistas, secret caves, and mysteries beyond human fathoming. Berry illuminates the character of this arduous journey in his essay:

> And the world cannot be discovered by a journey of miles, no matter how long, but only by a spiritual journey . . . it is a journey we can make only by the acceptance of mystery and of mystification—by yielding to the condition that what we have experienced is not there.[73]

ROMANCES

Romance (N.): Fiction that owes no allegiance to
the God of things as They Are.
—AMBROSE BIERCE

In his figurative scenes, including the gorge photographs, Meatyard applied the same techniques he used in his abstracted work. Formal means—reflected and indirect as well as direct light, blurring, composition, texture, shift of focal plane, and multiple exposure—join figures and props to become carriers of narrative and symbolic content. Produced throughout his career, Meatyard's figurative works are romances as Ambrose Bierce defined the genre: stories that need never actually have taken place to ring true. Like a wizard, Meatyard transmuted the drab banality of ruined houses, dime store masks, and hooded sweatshirts into disturbingly stark surrealist dramas.

The devices he used to effect this transformation include deliberate ambiguity and paradox, which are Zen teaching tools. Many of Meatyard's photographs can be considered koans—deliberately paradoxical questions or riddles used to free the mind from logic on the path to enlightenment. He employed qualities that Merton described as classic Zen material: "curious anecdotes, strange happenings . . . explosions of illogical humor, not to mention contradictions, inconsistencies, eccentric and even absurd behavior . . . aimed at blasting the foundation of ready explanation and comforting symbol out from the disciple's supposed 'experience.' "[74] Meatyard's humor and grotesqueries masked serious messages that could not be stated plainly; the world seemed far too complex and uncertain for direct means or definitive proclamations. Instead, Meatyard devised koanlike scenes that are a cross between parables and paradoxes.

The principal subject of these Zen sermons is the strenuous and perilous voyage from youth to old age to death. Included under this rubric is the topic of relationships between parent and child, adult and youth. Although the models were Meatyard's own family, the stories are not biographical anecdotes: they are ritualized encounters in dramatic settings. The framing of such scenes often recalls theater's proscenium arch. Although these images seem to be removed from actual incidents in Meatyard's own life, they do speak strongly of their environment. Most of them were made in the 1960s, a period of pronounced generational strife and social dislocation that had its impact on the Meatyard home as it did on most of American society. The struggles Meatyard shows were made at a time when relationships between young and old, parent and child, were especially discordant. Other photographers of the period, from Diane Arbus to Larry Clark to Bruce Davidson, addressed this same alienation through different styles and themes.[75]

The subject of a number of Meatyard's dramas is the state of childhood. One view of childhood is that of a time free of cares and full of curiosity. Though rare, there are Meatyard photographs that capture the exuberance of youth. Their protagonists are usually female; often it is the artist's daughter, Melissa, who poses. In *Untitled* (p. 122), a young girl is caught in the act of whirling around, sheer physical pleasure visible in her smile. An old, roughly textured shed darkened by a mysterious shadow contrasts with her sun-drenched figure. Melissa is one of two girls seen in *Untitled* (p. 123), where the intimacy and happiness of childhood friendships are explored. The image, showing bare feet, leafy vines, and glistening sunlight, is redolent of summer ease. The girls on a porch swing, facing each other and ignoring the camera, laugh uproariously at some private joke. Their laughter and perhaps the motion of the porch swing blur their figures, which express their physical as well as psychic involvement in this moment of mirth.

The rosy view of childhood characterizes it as a time of unbounded optimism and imagination. Children often play by imagining that the ordinary is really something magical; Meatyard himself never lost that ability. In *Untitled* (Child with hubcap; p. 41) from about 1959, a young boy in a field touches a hovering circular object, its metallic surface ringed with grooves and its edges eaten away by shadows. Darkness shades all but the child's hands, the flowers, and the top of the magical object. The boy's lower body is not visible, as if he, like the object, is floating. He touches the circle lightly and rapidly, seemingly aware of its power. The viewer is left wondering about the next moment, once the circle has worked its magic. Will a genie arise? Will the object take off and swoop up into

UNTITLED [Child with hubcap], c. 1959

the stratosphere? Will the child change in size, like Alice in Wonderland when she ate bites off different sides of the magic mushroom?[76] The circle, in truth, was no wondrous thing but only a lost hubcap, its grooves mere scratches and scars.

Props such as the hubcap were frequently the gifts of chance—found objects. Meatyard also had a collection of objects that he sometimes carried with him in his car. The miscellany varied at different times but could include masks, dead birds, or baby dolls. (In the late 1960s, Meatyard incorporated these and other objects into assemblages meant to hang on a wall as sculptures.[77]) Usually relying on the inspiration of the moment rather than any predetermined plan, he would arrive at a concept for an image and arrange the objects and models accordingly. Having decided on precisely the image he wanted, Meatyard would then instruct the models (his family and friends) how and where to stand, detailing when, how far, and how fast to move a hand or turn a head. When it came time to print, which was often over six months later, he would "read" the negatives to choose the best shots.

In these figurative shots, when Meatyard was not documenting a magical moment in the life of a child, he was creating an illusion. Each image is a staged scene, with the darks, highlights, and motions thought out in the photographer's mind in advance. The work is fiction—the antithesis of the work of "street photographers" such as Garry Winogrand and Lee Friedlander. Lionized by much of the photographic world as the height of photography in the 1960s, the street photographers caught people in unposed situations and unguarded moments. These "slices of life" commented on the society at large and on human nature. While the artists realized and worked with the fact that the camera's eye was a mediated and controlled one, their work relied on the photograph's sense of authenticity in portraying the real world. Meatyard, on the other hand, dealt with a reality that was above or beyond the familiar physical world, often discussing his work as "superreal" and "surreal." Familiar with surrealist art from his reading, he consciously drew on its odd juxtapositions, dreamlike quality, and sense of dislocation or alienation. Unlike the surrealists, Meatyard demanded that all the elements in his picture exist in the real world. In his notes, Meatyard urged himself to "take advantage of truth to make illusion and illusion to make truth."[78]

As is true of literary fiction, Meatyard's photographic fictions most often depict a conflict of some kind. His portrait of a young girl, *Untitled* (p. 128), presents a blur, the result of the model's slight motion, which becomes almost a tremor. Although she gazes at the viewer, her expression communicates uncertainty and a degree of wariness. Hers is a confined image, reinforced by the containment of her pose and bounded by a chalk rectangle sketched on the canvas background. The freedom and confidence in the two images of girls discussed above are absent here; this is childhood constrained by self-doubt as well as by external restrictions.

A number of Meatyard's works address the gradual but inevitable transition from childhood to adulthood. An emblem of this state is the child with an adult mask—a head too large on a body too small. Masks are common props in Meat-yard's photographs. These dime store or magic store masks, neither elaborate nor precious, bear idiotic grins, physical deformities, flayed skin, or exaggerated features. On a child at Halloween these masks might be scary or mocking. In Meatyard's images, they assume a compassionate air. The boy in *Untitled* (Sitting boy with mask and masked hands; p. 44) poses patiently, tilting his oversized pumpkinlike head in a reflective pose. His enormous hands would be folded in his lap, but they are too big, so they hang over onto a rock. This pose brings to mind the physical awkwardness of a teenage boy whose limbs have grown too quickly for the rest of his body to adjust. This portrait of a Franken-stein made of mismatched parts—one tamed and sadly aware of his own gro-tesqueness—calls forth sympathy, not horror.

In *Romance (N.) From Ambrose Bierce #3* (p. 61), masks transform seemingly ordinary children sitting on bleacher steps into hybrid child/adults. (The child at the bottom of the picture wears the mask that would become Lucybelle Crater from 1969 to 1972.) The disjunction of the oversized ears and noses of old age atop young bodies prophesies inevitable aging accompanied by suffering and sadness. Growing old is a morbid joke indeed. This macabre quality is rein-forced by a lighter, if somewhat diabolical, note sounded by a small, leering mask in the upper right-hand corner. The children's poses suggest resignation, contemplation, or even boredom. Juxtaposed against these emotionally loaded figures is a rational, orderly, and purely intellectual construct—numbers count-ing off each tier of seats. The masks seem to add the weight of the world onto the children's shoulders. Disguised, they lose their specific identity to be-come symbolic figures conflating the opposite ends of the life cycle—youth and old age.

In *Romance*, masks transform, but they can also disguise and conceal. A quo-tation in Meatyard's notes discusses this possibility:

> Our ritual face is not the person we "really" are, but rather the image we want other people to have of us, our persona, the mask we wear, the role we want to play. This perspective sees every brief encounter as a masked dance; it infuses everyday life with a sacred, a magical power.[79]

The young boy climbing a sheer wall of rock (p. 142) wears not one but two faces, one on his hip and one on the back of his head. As he proceeds on his perilous ascent (to adulthood?) he shows two faces to the world, neither of which is his own. The positions of the masks are humorous, yet the overall mes-sage is chilling. Behind the ritual masks, one's true identity is preoccupied by the real matter of living, the struggle. This is a grim view of life; not even the masks are smiling.

The impossibility of seeing through another's mask, of breaking through rit-ualized relationships to the true self is apparent in a number of Meatyard's pho-tographs that employ physical barriers to symbolize psychological distance be-tween people. His two sons, wife, and daughter most often serve as the models for these images. Architectural elements isolate Meatyard's sons in *Untitled* (p. 131). One boy is set back against a wall, his body almost filling the right third

UNTITLED [Sitting boy with mask and masked hands], 1960

of the frame. Only the head and shoulders of the other boy occupy the foreground at the lower left of the picture. Between them juts the strong diagonal of a bannister. Meatyard enhanced their separation by associating each figure with different tonal values, one dark against light and the other, the reverse. Shadows encroach upon the brightly lit head of the bust-length figure, turning his face into a kind of mask. Meatyard has deliberately obscured the boys' identities through shadow, the blur caused by motion, and the shallow depth of field that throws the foreground head out of focus. This image may or may not reflect the boys' actual relationship. This it not necessarily their story; it is Meatyard's drama.

Similarly ritualized encounters occur in a number of images of Meatyard's wife, Madelyn, and daughter, Melissa. Some indicate unbreachable separation between youth and adult. In an untitled work from 1970–71 (p. 134), the two occupy opposite ends of a barren room and are separated by the enclosed walls of a staircase. In their poses they mirror each other yet, at the same time, offer opposition. Each holds her hands up, but while the woman's hand moves, the girl's is still. The girl shakes her head, blurring its features, while the woman stares intently at the camera. Meatyard uses perspective and setting to invert the normal size relationship. The girl, because she is in the foreground, has a much larger body than the woman, who is set back and also has descended a few steps.

By contrast, *Madonna* of 1964 (p. 135) is an image of adoration and intimacy. Silhouetted against an arched window, the mother and child are physically bonded: the young girl's face rests against the woman's womb. A Venetian blind sags to highlight the woman's classical profile; her pose has the graceful beauty of Renaissance madonnas. Light not only outlines the figures but also blesses their relationship. Again, Meatyard portrays a schematic rather than a natural gesture. The rigid dignity and restraint of the mother's pose, while quite different from Madelyn's own vivacious personality, recall art historical and Christian visual tradition. Despite such references, Meatyard's is a secular interpretation, a paean to motherhood rather than to religion.

Physical intimacy can accompany an act of aggression as well as one of adoration. In a ruined house, a masked girl kneels beside a masked woman who gestures upward (p. 133). The girl looks up at the camera as if surprised by it. The two masked faces touch, as do their bodies, but it is unclear whether this is a display of affection or whether the child is attacking the woman. As in *Madonna*, the players are set in the center of the picture. The flatness of the symbols in *Madonna* is replaced here by a stagelike setting, with the picture's edge forming a proscenium arch. Camera and viewer become the audience in this drama.

An awareness of human mortality prevails in Meatyard's figurative scenes. References to death are frequent, beginning with the 1955 documentary series of tombstones. Two years later Meatyard returned to photographing funerary statuary. These later cemetery pictures, which he continued to make through 1960, are as expressive and metaphorical as the earlier ones are literal and factual. In *Untitled* (Cemetery Statue) of 1959 (p. 94), an angel cradles the deceased in a touching embrace suggestive of a Pietà. Though eroded by the elements, the figures retain a certain grace and allure. By heightening the contrast of dark and light and eliminating many of the middle tones, Meatyard exaggerates the statue's decay which in turn calls to mind the body in the unseen grave below. The result is a gentle and metaphorical rather than horrific representation of death.

Meatyard's photographs treat the illness of his friend and fellow photographer Cranston Ritchie without sentimentality. Ritchie lost first his hand, then his arm, and eventually his life to cancer. Meatyard posed Ritchie, whose arm at this point had been replaced by a hook, opposite a legless, armless mannequin (p. 153). Ritchie's lack of expression and matter-of-fact pose suggest his acceptance of the probable decay of his body as predicted by the mannequin. Meatyard interposed a cryptic symbol between the two bodies—a mirror reflecting a pure, bright light. The viewer is left wondering if this light represents the life force, the afterlife, or just the unknown.

Symbols of death are often juxtaposed with children in Meatyard's pictures. In one image from around 1962 (p. 137), a naked toddler stands beside a skull—really a mask—summing up the journey of life. In another photograph (p. 136), a tool that resembles a scythe but is actually a pickax hovers menacingly over a young boy. He wears a knitted cap that joins the neckline of his jacket to form the appearance of a hood. This hood and the shadows that partially obscure his features suggest that he may be a young version of the Grim Reaper. The wildly patterned floral wallpaper that serves as the background argues for life, as does the youth of the figure, but the blade that hangs above pronounces a death sentence, however far in the future it may come.

Although decay and death are biological facts, memories and spiritual presences offer a chance for preservation and commemoration. Such are the goals of the cemetery markers that Meatyard photographed. While the rotting, abandoned structures seen in many of his pictures are reminders of the passing of all things, they also testify to the past existence of their builders and inhabitants. Some of these structures may be preserved and renewed by future generations, as was the case for several sites that Meatyard photographed.[80] Restoring old houses was, after all, his father's occupation.

In numerous images, Meatyard proposes the possibility that the spirit persists after death. Though this is not a visible phenomenon, he causes the camera's eye to suggest such presences. In an image from about 1966 (p. 149), one of Meatyard's sons holds a fragment of mirror in front of his face, and it seems as if the boy has been caught in the act of materializing—or dematerializing. The section of wall that arches above his body bears written reminders of past visitors' attempts to gain some small measure of immortality. In other works, ghosts are summoned by the techniques of multiple exposure and blurring through motion. The transparent woman who wanders through a ruined mansion is seen twice, coming and going, unaware of the intruder (the camera/viewer) who watches her through the door (p. 47). Van Deren Coke described such images as the "reveries of a wandering soul."[81] Neither sadness nor pity, salvation nor damnation, are suggested in these images, merely acceptance. As Meatyard declared in his notes, "It is."

UNTITLED [Two ghosts with fireplace], c. 1969

Meatyard was extraordinarily conscious of his own mortality when he made the ghostly images. In 1961, at age thirty-six, he suffered a serious heart attack that immobilized him for half a year. The first photographs dealing with mortality, however, predate his heart attack; the boy with the scythe was made in 1960. In 1970, Meatyard was diagnosed with terminal cancer. He never gave up living despite this grim prognosis. He continued to work in his shop, visit his friends, and create new photographs long after the doctors had predicted he would die.

LUCYBELLE CRATER AND LUCYBELLE CRATER

Do a book of pictures and writing called "The Absence of John Jacob Niles"—shooting places he was . . . and things he did . . . , of course after he dies. Sort of a biography.

—RALPH EUGENE MEATYARD

Meatyard's final series, The Family Album of Lucybelle Crater, is his most enigmatic. He began it before he learned he had cancer, but most of the work was done during his two-year illness.[82] Some critics find the series repetitive or consider it a private joke. Those who think it significant often interpret it differently, some categorizing it as intellectual and others as emotional. Van Deren Coke felt the series was a literary idea carried out in pictorial terms. Meatyard's friend and fellow photographer Robert May called it "Meatyard's last sermon on the use of the mask, preaching like an old-fashioned Southern Baptist preacher for going to hell."[83] If one becomes personally acquainted with the individuals who constitute Lucybelle's "family," elements of tenderness and even sentimentality begin to manifest themselves in the series. The ambiguity of the series allows for the possibility that all these opposing views are valid.

The photographs pair Meatyard's wife, Madelyn, who appears in each picture, with one of his friends or family members. The two figures are set in the informal but staged poses one might find in a family album. The backgrounds sometimes relate specifically to the sitter, but more often include emblems of suburbia: modest homes, somewhat scraggly lawns, and immaculately kept cars. These scenes have a matter-of-fact, "real-life" quality that distinguishes them from the dramas discussed above. Jarring the viewer from suburban normalcy are the subjects' masks. The second figure, who changes in each photograph, wears a transparent mask that partially assumes the features of the person wearing it while making them appear older than they actually are. Meatyard described it as allowing you to see the person forty years from now.[84] Madelyn's opaque mask depicts an old woman with exaggerated, oversized, sad features—the Lucybelle Crater of the title.

Lucybelle Crater is not just a random selection from Meatyard's collection of odd names but was adapted from a short story entitled "The Life You Save May Be Your Own" by the Southern author Flannery O'Connor, whose writing Meatyard greatly enjoyed.[85] In O'Connor's story, an old woman introduces both herself and her idiot daughter as Lucynell Crater. This sharing of a single name may be a female version of naming one's son junior or it may mock the odd family structures and verbal impoverishment of the rural Southern poor. Meatyard, who wrote captions on an exhibition set of Lucybelle photographs, identified each of the people who posed with Madelyn as also bearing the name Lucybelle Crater.[86]

Meatyard chose his sources in as eclectic and eccentric a way as he selected his reading material. There is little connection between the plot of the story and the specific content of the photographs: O'Connor writes about a rotten world where a dishonest drifter marries the daughter only to abandon her. Meatyard's imminent though unwilling abandonment of his "family" may be the only link between the two. Another literary source more directly connected to the series is Gertrude Stein's essay "Portraits and Repetitions." In Meatyard's series, the repetitive format and recurrent masks—varied by changes in background, pose, and personnel—resembles the repetition and variation in Stein's written portraits.

Meatyard and Stein also shared a desire to create "portraits of any one," as Stein put it.[87] The masks disguise the identity of each Lucybelle, transforming him or her into "everyperson" just as a Zen Twig stood for the entire tree or even for the forest. Meatyard's family and friends become a representation of the universal family, stocked with several generations of the near, the dear, and the distantly associated. Lucybelle's family is the Family of Man (and Woman), the universal family.[88]

Nonetheless, each body reveals a separate person through clothes, stance, size, gesture, and other unmistakable traits, and the transparent mask changes radically with each wearer. The conflation of individualism with generic type is reflected in the titles of the works, where the person's relationship is made clear. *Lucybelle Crater & 20 yr old son's 3 yr old son, also her 3 yr old grandson—Lucybelle Crater* (p. 179), for example, is a poignant image of an old-faced woman stooping down beside her grandson. Standing in a bed of fallen leaves, they represent not just three generations of Meatyard's family but also the cycle of life from youth to old age to death. This is the artist's, the viewer's, anyone's family album.

Often in family albums, one person assumes the role of the photographer and is absent from most of the shots. The person's presence, however, is implicit in each image because the subjects all look toward the photographer. Meatyard's presence is very much in evidence in the Lucybelle series. Three photographs in this series contain his image. In *LBC and Eastern man's friend, LBC* (p. 177), Van Deren Coke stands on the steps of a front porch with Lucybelle (Madelyn) behind and above him. The dark shadow of the photographer covers the lower half of Coke's figure. Meatyard modestly places his own image much lower than the body of his mentor. This causes the shadow of his head to fall on the stomach of the man who is responsible for his birth as an artist in a statement of homage and farewell.

For the other two photographs, which begin and end the series, Meatyard used a self-timer. With their feet covered by a snarl of garden hose, "Lucybelle Crater and her 40 yr old husband Lucybelle Crater" (p. 176) stand between an oak and a redbud tree in the first image. This suburban Adam and Eve, an archetypal couple, do not touch. His hands are in his pockets while her arms are crossed. Wearing slightly different clothes, the same figures stand between the poles of a grape arbor in the final image of the series, *Lucybelle Crater And Close Friend Lucybelle Crater In The Grape Arbor* (p. 183). Lucybelle the old woman addresses the male Lucybelle with some urgency, touching him on the shoulder and bringing her face close to his ear. He ignores her to look at the camera. There is something oddly but subtly disturbing about this picture. The figures, out of kilter as they list slightly to the left, seem less at home in their bodies and more artificially posed. Without extremely close examination, though, it is difficult to guess what is wrong with this picture: Lucybelle Crater has switched clothes and places with Lucybelle Crater. Meatyard, having lost weight because of cancer, fit himself into his wife's clothes and donned the solid mask. His wife, dressed in his clothes, wore the transparent one. This subtle joke is yet another level of mask.

The Family Album of Lucybelle Crater is Meatyard's summary of his life. He chose not to show the places he had been or the things he had done, this man whose life was most real in the realm of the imagination. Instead he presented his kin, whether related by blood, marriage, or friendship; his intellectual life and love of literature; and his belief in the power of truthful illusion. The spirituality prevalent in the early work is largely absent, perhaps because the fact of mortality is so present. The Lucybelle series, like all of Meatyard's work, has several faces, several layers of meaning. It is personal and universal, erudite and folksy, tragic and witty. Behind Meatyard's work lay a profound spirit, one that delighted in the often contradictory nature of his art and his very existence.

CONCLUSION

Meatyard died in 1972. Shortly after his death, several exhibitions were organized; two books and a portfolio of his photographs were published. At the time, a sense of loss prevailed and his work was still steeped in the time of its creation. Now, almost two decades later, it is time for a re-examination. The characteristics of his work that gave his contemporaries the most difficulty are those that seem most relevant to contemporary photography and painting. Meatyard's emphasis on drama, gesture, and emotion in his abstract work was very much at odds with art of the 1960s and 1970s, but is present in the paintings of a number of artists working today in abstract surrealist and expressionist styles. The past few years has also seen renewed interest in abstract photography, with exhibitions surveying its history—some of which included Meatyard's work—as well as examining contemporary abstract photography.

Meatyard's fabricated or staged figurative images are even more closely related to contemporary art practice. Today a number of artists set up and photograph staged scenes, including Cindy Sherman, who, like Meatyard, use masks and other props to create mysterious fictional identities and dramas. These artists, many of whom are not trained as photographers, share Meatyard's lack of concern for the tradition of the fine photographic print. They may reproduce the blurring that comes from photographing motion at a slow exposure or, like Richard Prince, produce deliberately out-of-focus images.[89]

Meatyard's delight in enigmatic, unresolvable images allies him with contemporary artists such as Sherman, Prince, Jeff Wall, and others known as postmodernists. All have abandoned modernism's forward-looking optimism and certainty. Instead, they project a sense of pessimism or distress. Their purposeful ambiguity suggests the impossibility of obtaining clear answers and establishing absolute values. Meatyard's is a detached stance that has a strongly personal base: it comes from his belief in Zen as well as from his own personality. The postmodernists, on the contrary, derive their pessimism from societal forces and use it to critique aspects of contemporary life.

Meatyard may not have directly inspired these younger artists. Nonetheless, his work, which was and is widely known by photographers and other artists, sets the stage for theirs. More significant than Meatyard's influence on future art is the impact his photographs continue to have on viewers. Whether abstract or figurative, the images clearly belong to a single eye and sensibility, one that relished beauty but was equally seduced by grotesqueness. Meatyard saw these two qualities forming not a continuum but a circle. Life is depicted in his photographs as an arduous but worthwhile journey and the world as a darkness—but one blessed with light.

UNTITLED [Series of three self-portraits with artist walking over hill], 1972

David L. Jacobs

Seeing the Unseen, Saying the Unsayable: On Ralph Eugene Meatyard

INTRODUCTION

When Ralph Eugene Meatyard died in May 1972 he left a partially developed roll of film in his camera. He had fought cancer for some time, and though he was getting progressively worse, he continued to photograph, socialize, and work in his optical store, Eyeglasses of Kentucky. Meatyard never disguised his condition from family or friends, but, as was his custom about much of his inner life, he remained in large part silent about the disease.

Sometime near the end of his life, he exposed his last film, three consecutive self-portraits made with the camera resting upon the ground. The scene is a hillside covered with rough grass and weed stalks. A single leafless tree stands on top of the hill. In the first picture Meatyard is seated beyond the crest of the hill looking back at the camera, with most of the lower part of his body out of sight. The second exposure shows him walking over the hill, his face turned back toward the camera. There are grass and weeds out of focus in the bottom foreground of the first two pictures. In the third picture he is walking in the same direction, this time looking down and away from the camera. He has slightly shifted the camera on the ground, thereby raising the weeds from the bottom part of the picture and replacing them with out-of-focus rocks. Meatyard didn't live to finish the roll, but after his friend and fellow photographer Robert May developed and printed it, Meatyard's friends and family saw in these final three pictures an appropriate coda. Wendell Berry concludes his reminiscence of Meatyard later in this book by suggesting that these pictures "were his elegy and farewell, and their impact was physical. . . . He had been going away from us as he now revealed himself to us: fully knowing, full in the light, though, as the near horizon showed, there would be an end of seeing."[1]

I never knew Ralph Eugene Meatyard, never ate his homemade violet jam or donned a mask as his model. I approach him, nearly twenty years after his death, as a historian, curator, and photographer, having sorted through thousands of prints, several interviews with friends and family, copies of virtually every article and essay written about his work, much of his library, and the relatively few letters and other writings that he left behind. Let me state at the outset that many aspects of Ralph Eugene Meatyard's life and art remain a mystery, despite all of my efforts.

For me, these three final self-portraits constitute a statement of Meatyard's ongoing fascination with process and discovery—central features of his explorations with photography, ideas, and life itself. The *process* of photography—of seeing and knowing the world and self through the mediation of the camera—interested him more than the final prints themselves. This passion for process was one of Meatyard's defining characteristics, present in the mechanical, nuts-and-bolts aspects of his photography as well as in his most spiritual, Zen-inspired musings.

When Parkinson's disease made it impossible for Edward Weston to continue to photograph, he conscripted his sons to print several hundred of his finest negatives. These so-called Project Prints represented Weston's efforts to establish his legacy. Meatyard, by contrast, did not devote his last months to tying up photographic loose ends. Throughout his career he seldom reprinted old negatives, and when he did so it was usually because they had been requested specifically for exhibition. Even as his body deteriorated—he would show family and friends how much more of his belt wrapped around his shrinking waistline—Meatyard continued to photograph until the very end of his life. What was past was past. The kick for him came from what could next be seen and known through the camera. His best work always lay in front of him, beyond the crest of the hill. As scholar and poet Guy Davenport remembers, "To Gene's mind there was always something more than what the rest of the world saw, and he was determined to go that extra inventive probe."[2]

How to do justice to this sense of process? How to know, much less represent the processes that generated the 115 or so images that grace the pages of this book? Inevitably, these prints, these *products,* however evocative and (we hope) well chosen, do not fully reveal the character of the artist and the various external forces that molded him. Even the most alert eyes can focus only on what is set before them; yet the spaces between these images—the soundless, crucial spaces that mediate Meatyard's vision, and indeed, that mediate all of our ways of seeing and knowing—remain in large part beyond our reckoning. Process—photographic, interpersonal, creative, spiritual—will be a recurrent theme in this essay, much as it was for Meatyard in his life and art.

PHOTOGRAPHIC CONTEXTS

In photography, control and accident are inevitable parts of the creative process. One of the great pleasures of the medium, whether for the haughtiest art photographer or the humblest snapshooter, is the sense of order that is gained when the world at large is captured within the neat right angles of a viewfinder. When standing before a larger-than-life vista we gain some measure of control, however illusory, by framing it within the confines of a picture that can be held in the palm of the hand. This act of selection is the crux of photography, for it determines not only what we get in the picture, but it signifies, more subtly, how we know ourselves and our relations to the world. Searching through the viewfinder—so modest and familiar an occurrence—we can restructure the everyday realities that surround us. This is as true for a snapshooter, who waits for what seems like hours before snapping the shutter at a Thanksgiving feast, as it was for Gene Meatyard, who organized his family and friends amid dolls and masks in broken-down houses. In seizing from the flux of life a photographic moment, we feel that we possess it in some small measure. The photographer or snapshooter looks through the viewfinder at a miniaturized, framed world, waiting for something to materialize that conforms to the world seen in the inner eye.

Meatyard maintained that he knew what he had captured on film at the moment he made the exposure. Previsualizing the final result before snapping the shutter is relatively easy when making portraits and tableaux, in which models are painstakingly posed. But Meatyard made the same claims for his more abstract work: the multiple exposures; the time exposures that result in blurred moving objects; the No-Focus work, in which the entire picture is purposefully cast out of focus; the studies of light reflected on water. Even with such highly abstract work, Meatyard claimed a full measure of previsualization—of knowing at the moment of taking the picture precisely what he had captured. Regarding the Light on Water photographs, for example, he wrote in 1970:

> Light changes all the time, but with [the Light on Water abstractions] . . . I got so that I would actually plot them out ahead of time by the use of multiple exposure, a moving camera and a light spectrum moving downstream as the sunlight is shining upon it. And whether the camera is at one part of focus or another would make the little dots either finer, sharper or bigger, blobbier. . . . I would then take an idea of what I wanted in the picture. I would know.[3]

When posing his models Meatyard could be highly dictatorial. His was not a "go-over-there-and-mess-around" style; instead he carefully positioned props and models, an exercise that could be not a little exhausting and exasperating for the models. But the very nature of the Light on Water and the No-Focus abstractions precludes the same degree of control, Meatyard's claims notwithstanding. Accident and serendipity are inevitable during picture making. However controlled the site of picture making—even in artificially lit studios where the variables are minimized—the photographer can be surprised by what the camera catches that the eye has missed. This is even more obvious in less controlled situations when facial expressions change, people move, and clouds block sunlight—when the unexpected intervenes. And the sheer plenitude of details that a camera captures prevents any photographer from seeing all of what is there.

The photographer can previsualize only so far, and beyond that he has little choice but to give himself over to accident. In these cases the photographer can learn a good deal about the medium and its possibilities precisely *because* the controls are relaxed. In Meatyard's No-Focus photographs, for example, the entire picture is thrown out of focus to the point that the viewer has little or no idea what was originally set before the lens. These images present ephemeral forms that only a camera can detect and transcribe. Their formalism should be seen in the larger context of experimenting with the camera's potential beyond its obvious capacity to record the details of whatever scene is set before it. In some of these images the dreamlike, primordial shapes can surprise us, and perhaps they surprised Meatyard too, down to the bone.

Meatyard was hardly alone in promoting the idea of previsualization. From the mid-1950s onward, claims for previsualization were made by many art photographers, some of whom were also experimenting with abstract photography. In the late 1940s and early 1950s, Ansel Adams developed the Zone System, a technical system of predetermining "zones" of gray through a careful combination of light readings, exposures, and developing times in the darkroom. Adams's definition emphasizes the element of control that the Zone System affords:

> A framework for understanding exposure and development, and visualizing their effect in advance. . . . Careful exposure and development procedures permit the photographer to control the negative densities and corresponding print values that will represent specific subject areas, in accordance with the visualized final image.[4]

Adams's work, in turn, was revised and published by Minor White in his influential *Zone System Manual,* in which previsualization is the crucial concept. As White wrote at the beginning of his book:

> The amateur who realizes that he is the victim of his equipment and materials can discover in the zone system a positive means of mastering his medium. . . . Hence, this manual is for those who want more out of photography than is popularly practiced; those who want to explore and extend their expressive-creative ability . . . Previsualization in practice can lead the photographer to work freely in any mode of the expressive creative [*sic*]. . . .[5]

The Zone System was more than a technical program for exposure and development: it was a subtle response to claims recurrent since the medium's invention that photography was a mere mechanical process, and thus not an art. The Zone System provided the photographer with control over black-and-white materials, and this element of control in turn contributed to the argument for accepting photography seriously as an art form. Some photographers explored the medium as a means for personal expression, while others spoke of wanting to discover a "grammar" or a "syntax" that was unique to photographic representation. In addition, a fair amount of photographic experimentation with abstraction was beholden to postwar developments in painting, particularly the work of the abstract expressionists and their heirs, although photographers were not always willing to own up to this painterly influence. Photographers such as Aaron Siskind, Harry Callahan, Minor White, Nathan Lyons, Walter Chappell, Henry Holmes Smith, and Wynn Bullock combined the claims for control with experiments in abstraction—both ambitions contributing to the overarching argument for taking photography seriously as a fine art.[6]

These were ideas that Meatyard understood and propounded. Like Weston, Adams, White, the Newhalls, and others, Meatyard was devoted to promoting photography as a fine art and himself as a serious artist. Particularly in the mid- to late 1950s, Meatyard came to understand many of these principles from his teacher, Van Deren Coke, who had a formative influence on Meatyard in a variety of ways. In the mid-1950s Meatyard and Coke worked together on a documentary project in which each photographed a separate side of Georgetown Street, a predominantly black neighborhood in Lexington.[7] Only a few years after Meatyard started photographing, Coke served as curator for the Lexington Camera Club exhibition "Creative Photography—1956," which included works by Ansel Adams, Ruth Bernhard, Wynn Bullock, Harry Callahan, Van Deren Coke, Ralph Eugene Meatyard, Arnold Newman, Charles Sheeler, Aaron Siskind, Edward Weston, and Minor White, each of whom was represented by ten prints. Clearly, Meatyard kept very good company from his earliest days in photography. The exhibition comprised an impressive rundown of then-young talent and suggested the astuteness of Coke's curatorial eye.

In 1956 Meatyard and Coke attended a workshop at Indiana University, where Meatyard first met Henry Holmes Smith and Minor White. One year later Meatyard and Coke exhibited together in New York at A Photographer's Gallery. Although only his second exhibition, Meatyard found his work favorably reviewed in the *New York Times,* where Jacob Deschin, after noting that Coke was Meatyard's teacher, added:

> A comparison of the two groups of pictures is valuable only as it points up the importance of true influence as opposed to imitation. Both photographers are concerned with good design and technique as well as their need to say something worthwhile. Beyond these essentials of valid photography, the photographers part company.[8]

Coke shared his growing print collection with his young student, and thus Meatyard came to the medium with the advantage of seeing original prints from many of the country's leading photographers. Well into the 1960s Coke put Meatyard in touch with his widening circle of friends and acquaintances in the field, thereby opening doors for more exhibitions and publications. Meatyard would have been hard pressed to find a more sophisticated or provocative mentor in New York or San Francisco.

After Van Deren Coke left Lexington to study at Indiana University late in 1956, there was no one in residence who knew as much about photography as

UNTITLED [Van Deren Coke and chandelier reflected in a mirror], c. 1955–57

Meatyard, though there were others who influenced him intellectually and spiritually. But it would be a mistake to think Meatyard was working in complete photographic isolation after Coke's departure. He continued to read photographic literature, sparse as it then was. And by curating three major exhibitions at the progressive Lexington Camera Club, in 1968, 1970, and 1972, he stayed in touch with cutting-edge work by young photographers from across the country. His print collection, most of which was accumulated through swapping prints, included photographs by Doris Ulmann, Emmet Gowin, Roger Mertin, Minor White, Paul Caponigro, and Robert Heinecken. Meatyard also had extended conversations with Nathan Lyons in the mid-1960s, and he found a kindred spirit in Frederick Sommer, whose work he held in the highest esteem.[9]

Meatyard's stance toward the photographic mainstream as represented by Stieglitz, Strand, Weston, and Adams was ambivalent. On the one hand, he identified strongly with their tradition of straight photography. In 1961 he wrote of himself for *Art in America*:

> I adhere to the techniques of the earliest and most sincere workers of the camera—straight, unmanipulated pictures. That which I present is that which I see. However, I work a great deal in romantic-surrealist as well as abstract [sic] for I feel that "more real than real" is the special province of the serious photographer.[10]

At the same time, Meatyard disregarded some of straight photography's hallowed conventions. This is most evident in his printing. Much as he admired full-toned black-and-white prints, he was not primarily interested in producing such prints from his own negatives. Adams or Strand would sometimes labor for hours or even days striving for the ultimate print, but Meatyard would usually content himself with the first or second print from a negative and move on.[11] While printing, he often overlooked conventional truisms such as retaining details in the shadows, instead favoring deep, featureless blacks. Many of his prints rendered the rich, verdant forests and undergrowth of Kentucky in high-contrast photographs that all but eliminated the grays. Meatyard also purposefully photographed parts of the image out of focus, thereby working against the sharpness through the picture plane aesthetic championed by the "Group f/64" landscape photographers.[12] Meatyard's landscapes look very different from the full-toned, razor-sharp photographs that Weston, Adams, Cunningham, and others made.

Meatyard's printing habits were hardly pristine. Fixer was not thoroughly eliminated from many of his prints and over time this created brown discoloring of the images and deterioration of the paper. Even after archival procedures began to take hold in the mid-1960s, Meatyard continued to dry mount many of his prints and neglected to utilize methods that would assure longer life for his photographs, with the regrettable result that a sizable number of prints in his archive are visibly deteriorating. One cannot write off Meatyard's darkroom practices as instances of sloppiness or sloth. He was in many respects a highly organized, meticulous man, and he was quite capable of making high-quality prints. But Meatyard was in the main indifferent to darkroom work. Like Cartier-Bresson or Garry Winogrand,[13] he was more interested in making exposures than in seeing results. His heart lay more in process than in products.

In other ways, however, Meatyard was traditional, if not downright conservative in his views on photography. He had dutifully read all of the back issues of *Aperture* in 1962, and like many photographers of the period he devoured Weston's *Daybooks* as one of the few books that dealt with the creative process in photography. Meatyard had an intense dislike of color photography, feeling that it was a distant cousin to the purity of black and white. In reference to his black-and-white landscapes of the Red River Gorge, Meatyard said, "I just don't like color. Oh, there's no real prejudice. . . . They're still a long way from what you could do with black and white, making things believable out of it."[14] He added that in some ways he was trying to "do a thing kind of like some of these Sierra Club [color photographs] in black and white. I like the way they feel; I have a compassion [sic] for more or less straight photography."[15]

Meatyard also resisted the highly manipulated photographs of Jerry Uelsmann, who relied upon sandwich printing that utilized parts of several different negatives. Meatyard's jottings in the margins of the Uelsmann portfolios that appeared in Aperture in 1967 and 1970 are notably hostile. Not unlike other straight photographers in the tradition of P. H. Emerson and Stieglitz, Meatyard insisted that the photographer's job was to "get it in the camera," and he thought that Uelsmann's darkroom manipulations went against this traditional aesthetic. Meatyard considered Uelsmann's postvisualized images as a form of cheating, and in his estimation they were not true to the medium.

While hardly an arrogant man, Meatyard possessed a healthy ego when it came to his own work and its place in the history of photography. It is clear in his unpublished manuscript on the No-Focus images from the late 1950s and early 1960s that he considered this work to be a breakthrough, not just in personal terms but also in the larger framework of the medium's history. After asserting that photography is an art form, and that Weston, Strand, and Siskind were "originators [who] are also true to their medium," Meatyard discussed the history of his No-Focus work:

> As for what No-Focus has done and can do—it is freedom. . . . It is an art of visual acrobatics which result in acrobatic emotions and misgivings. No criticism has ever seemed as valid as the reasons for the importance of the being of No-Focus.
>
> My hopes and intentions for No-Focus are many. I see no limitations, no end, to the possibilities of this endeavor as long as abstraction does not take over the all important content of the picture. . . .
>
> I have been impressed by all forms of art. I feel that the image was predetermined centuries ago, and yet I feel along with Ben Shahn in that [sic] a great part of abstracted art represents only the rejections and self-commitment of the artist. Again, like Shahn, I believe that to make a picture is to intend; therefore to intend and not intend like so much abstracting [sic], is hopeless and yet much exhibited. The more universal anything is the more abstracted it must be. Averages and generalities are for the sentimentalists. The most universal might be some extreme limit of feelings—the unique thing which affirms the unique qualities of all things.
>
> I believe that in No-Focus I have begun to achieve this unique thing, and with further study will be able to further myself and it.[16]

Like many an artist, Meatyard wanted to be counted among his medium's movers and shakers. But he also possessed a sense of humor on the issue, as may be seen in the following anecdote. Beaumont Newhall was and perhaps still is the foremost American historian of photography. The first edition of his History of Photography was written in 1937 to accompany a major show presenting the medium's history at The Museum of Modern Art, and it has been revised several times since. When he discovered that he was not mentioned in the 1964 edition of Newhall's History—the first revision since 1949—Meatyard inserted himself

ROMANCE (N.) FROM AMBROSE BIERCE #3, 1962

into history by wryly dry mounting his *Romance (N.) From Ambrose Bierce #3* onto one of the blank pages in the front of Newhall's book.

One may account for the omission of Meatyard in various ways. By 1961 Newhall had enough regard for Meatyard's work to include him in an article in *Art in America* that featured promising young photographers.[17] But Newhall's history of this diverse medium ran a scant 200 pages, including illustrations. There were many stories to be told and many photographers had to be excluded. As we have seen, promoting photography as a fine art was a ruling passion for many photographers, including Meatyard, and appearing in a history of the medium that served this purpose was a central component to achieving success. Newhall was most drawn to the tradition of Stieglitz, Strand, and Weston, and they and their progeny are the heroes of his story. The concluding paragraph of Newhall's 1962 edition of the *History* succinctly sums up his position:

> More and more are turning to photography as a medium of expression as well as communication. The leavening of esthetic approaches which we have noted continues. While it is too soon to define the characteristic of the photographic style of today, one common denominator, rooted in tradition, seems in the ascendancy: the direct use of the camera for what it can do best, and that is the revelation, interpretation and discovery of the world of man and of nature. The greatest challenge to the photographer is to express the inner significance through the outward form.[18]

The photographs included in Newhall's final chapter, "Recent Trends," reveal the guiding aesthetic: there are two nature studies by Minor White; a landscape by Otto Steinert; two photographs by Siskind; a tree by Callahan; and Robert Frank's photograph of a tuba player. There was little room in Newhall's *History* for images that called into question the straight photography aesthetic or for images that conveyed social or political critique. With the exception of Robert Frank's photograph, none of the contemporary work included in this final chapter had any edge of social or political criticism, and the Frank picture that was included was one of his less biting images from *The Americans*.[19]

A major criterion was not only expressiveness, but expressiveness of a particular sort. The copious correspondence between Beaumont and Nancy Newhall and Ansel Adams during the mid-1950s makes clear their aversion to images that treated subject matter that was not conventionally beautiful or affirmative, whether Frederick Sommer's decaying animals or Robert Frank's grainy handheld portraits. The critical, questioning edge that was perceived in the work of Frank, Sommer, and others disturbed and possibly offended the Newhalls and Adams. In their view, not only did such work have questionable aesthetic merit, but it did not serve the agenda of promoting photography as an art.[20]

The palpable edge in much of Meatyard's work no doubt evoked similar responses. But Meatyard was in good company: absent from and unmentioned in the 1964 edition of Newhall's *History* were Helen Levitt, Lisette Model, Frederick Sommer, Sid Grossman, and many other photographers whose images confronted social realities and sometimes presented disturbing pictures of what lay beneath.[21]

Had Meatyard lived another ten years he would have had to dry mount yet another picture in order to enter the Newhall pantheon, since he does not appear in Newhall's 1982 revision of the *History*. The concluding paragraph of Newhall's 1982 edition is *identical* to the 1964 conclusion quoted above, as if nothing had changed in the intervening eighteen years. But Newhall is not the only American historian who neglects to give Meatyard significant attention. In 1989, several major exhibitions and accompanying catalogues were devoted to the history of photography in celebration of the 150th anniversary of its invention. However, no Meatyard photographs appear in *Photography Until Now*,[22] in *On the Art of Fixing the Shadow*,[23] or in *Decade by Decade*,[24] and only in this last book is Meatyard even mentioned. Among the major sesquicentennial publications, only Adam Weinberg's *Vanishing Presence*[25] features the work of Ralph Eugene Meatyard in a significant way.[26]

There are many reasons why Meatyard's reputation has suffered, some of which we have already touched upon. His photographs are challenging both aesthetically and psychologically, a contention that viewers and readers of this book will readily understand. There are optimistic, upbeat images, portraits, and landscapes in Meatyard's oeuvre, but the pictures that stay most vividly in mind are those that reach down into dangerous psychological territory. As Anne Hoy has written of Meatyard's Lucybelle Crater series, "If James Ensor had taken snapshots in [William Faulkner's] Yoknapatawpha County, the effect might have been similar: the disturbing quality of Meatyard's images derives not from his actors or places but, one feels, from his projection of personal terrors upon them."[27] And the fact that Meatyard is seen as a regional photographer from Kentucky has also played a role in his relatively low profile in recent years. In this regard, it is interesting to compare the reputations of Meatyard and Diane Arbus and to ponder how each might have fared had Meatyard been a New Yorker who was discovered by John Szarkowski and Arbus a Kentucky optician who photographed on the weekends.

I believe that another reason for historians' relative neglect of Meatyard is the sheer volume and diversity of his photographs. Meatyard restlessly experimented with various styles of photography in an effort to discover new ways of effecting self-expression, and this made him something of a photographer's photographer. He appealed to other intellectually inclined photographers such as Nathan Lyons, Minor White, Henry Holmes Smith, and Van Deren Coke—educators whose experimental work was difficult and relatively inaccessible to broad audiences. Although Meatyard's oeuvre is often associated with his photographs of children, masks, and dolls, it is important to remember that this versatile photographer pointed his camera at a considerable range of subjects throughout his career. As early as 1959, Van Deren Coke would call Meatyard a "most prolific artist," one who produced approximately two thousand exposures and six to seven hundred prints a year.[28] Meatyard would wait several months or even a year before developing a backlog of film in a two-week stretch, and he would do a year's worth of printing during that frantic fortnight.[29] He printed an exceptionally high percentage of exposures, often more than half of

Untitled [Still life: two masks hung in interior], c. 1961–62

each roll of film, and that accounts for the enormity of his archive—well over five thousand different prints, a considerable output for less than twenty years of photography.

Meatyard's subjects included architecture, cemetery headstones, children, friends, old walls, dilapidated houses, rushing water, urban sprawl, suburban kitsch, rural openness, and even a nude or two.[30] In a lecture delivered near the end of his life, Meatyard recounted that he had worked "in about 16 different styles throughout my photography and at any time I might return to one particular one, work it again, and develop a new one out of it."[31] While it is not unusual for young photographers to approach numerous subjects when they first begin using a camera, such diversity is quite rare for mature photographers, who typically settle into particular niches that they mine throughout the remainder of their lives. Meatyard, on the other hand, was able to photograph very different kinds of subject matter simultaneously. He experimented with abstract landscape studies throughout the 1960s, even as he was producing the surreal images that ensured his reputation. From the mid-1950s until his death he returned again and again to the Light on Water photographs, which include a series of eight abstractions entitled Pictures of Self. The best example of Meatyard's ability to work different veins simultaneously is seen in two of his most substantial bodies of work—the Red River Gorge landscapes that appeared in his book *The Unforeseen Wilderness* and the Lucybelle Crater photographs. These two sets of images were made concurrently between 1969 and 1971, and Meatyard continued to photograph in other registers during the same period as well. Very few photographers could embrace such apparently different styles at the same time. Indeed, his ability to work effectively across genres is a major reason why his work remains of such interest today.

Meatyard viewed himself in the tradition of modernist painters and writers who combine a strong belief in the underlying forms of nature and art with the view of the artist as someone who orders (or disrupts) the world-as-seen. He saw the camera as a means for converting sensory and optical data into the deeper imaginative and mythical dimensions of experience. As early as 1956 he wrote:

> I seek to create a picture that has implications which may be explored for a new concept in thinking—a picture seen largely from a subjective viewpoint. The man of ideas and ideals will search for and find elements of his imagination in segments of the actuality around him. My pictures are an extension of myself and invite the viewers to participate in my thinking about the object pictured.[32]

He was an unapologetic subjectivist, interested much more in metaphor than in metonymy. The challenge for Meatyard lay in translating states of consciousness into blacks, whites, and grays using a tool, the camera, that is ostensibly best suited for recording the surfaces of things. The poet and essayist Wendell Berry, who has lived in and farmed the Kentucky landscape for much of his life, remembers looking through Meatyard's Rolleiflex at lichen on an ash tree and being astonished that the image on the ground glass was so different from what he had first perceived. As Berry put it, "Framed by the camera, this altogether accountable sight became altogether unaccountable. It was unearthly, seeming to remove the ordinary elements of the vision out of ordinary time."[33]

Meatyard's landscapes are not concerned with the faithful representation of the "natural scene," as Ansel Adams often referred to it, but rather they are patently metaphorical and transformative. This is true not only of the No-Focus images but also of the more literal landscapes, such as the Red River prints, which contain areas so dark that they give no hint of details in the underbrush or rock outcroppings. Rather, they suggest a sense of void and absence that is akin to Edward Weston's last photographs of Point Lobos, with their intimations of mortality amid nature's plenty.

Meatyard enacted transformations of a different sort in one of his best-known series, The Family Album of Lucybelle Crater. In these photographs we find ordinary folks dressed in plain, homey clothes posing nonchalantly on the front porch, beside shady streets, or in front of hedges in the backyard. They seem wholly unaware of their grotesque faces. They pose as if for family pictures, which customarily present our most positive selves to our family and posterity. And they are, in a way, family pictures, since Meatyard's wife, Madelyn, was the model for Lucybelle throughout, with the single exception of the final image, *Lucybelle Crater And Close Friend Lucybelle Crater In The Grape Arbor* (p. 183), in which Meatyard himself, completely disguised in a mask and dress, poses as Lucybelle and Madelyn poses as the other figure.[34] Other models included friends such as Wendell Berry, Guy Davenport, Jonathan Greene, Emmet Gowin, Robert May, Charles Traub, and Van Deren Coke. Some of the pictures reflect the relationships that Meatyard had with his models in their "real life" occupations. As in many family albums, there are private references and jokes in these images, known only to a few of Meatyard's intimates.[35]

In spite of the title, the Lucybelle photographs are hardly what we think of as snapshots. They are much more closely related to the "snapshot aesthetic" that emerged in the late 1960s, as distinguished from the informal, technically naïve, and generally sunny images made by snapshooters. Meatyard's set-ups are infused with a brand of irony that is seldom encountered in family albums. If anything, the masks mock the omnipresent smiles and interpersonal niceties of typical family albums. The Lucybelle pictures have more in common with the sophisticated, ironic, deadpan images of Diane Arbus, Lee Friedlander, and Garry Winogrand[36] than with pictures of little Johnny blowing out birthday candles.

The formal repetition in this series runs the risk of redundancy, of a simple conceit taken to extremes. The central figure, Lucybelle, remains the constant while the scene itself shifts throughout a full range of informal, suburban settings inhabited by weird but friendly personages, all of whom stand beside her, converse with her, or interact with her in other ways. Meatyard uses repetition to present issues of identity and the multiplicity of the self.[37] With repeated viewings these images assume deeper meaning as the models seem to take on additional character traits. We recognize the masks on one hand as the products of artifice, while on the other hand we are free to read into them what we will.

And in turn, we are tempted to make narratives of these images, to find connections through stories of our making between the masks and the anomalous bodies beneath them, and, even more, to speculate about the relationships between the paired characters in the photographs.

When organizing these characters in the Kentucky landscape, Meatyard was working in a dramatic mode, directing friends and family, arranging the components of a family gathering into a *danse macabre* transformed into static black-and-white images. Meatyard stage-managed his cast of everymen, whose scuffed shoes and jeans spoke of the everydayness of the American middle class while the grimaces and twisted faces of the masks pointed to other psychic states. The ordinary is mixed with the extraordinary, banality with the grotesque, the comic with the tragic: the surrealism of everyday life. The Lucybelle series is surely comic, but the dislocation of its characters in time and place points to the tragic as well. The series is not unlike Shakespeare's so-called problem plays—most notably *The Tempest* with its shifts of mood and its remarkable combination of the comic and the tragic, the profane and the sacred. This backyard Prospero placed his Mirandas, Ferdinands, and Calibans in commonplace American settings that resonate with the ancient themes of love and betrayal, possession and loss, innocence and experience.

The Lucybelle photographs play off of these poles, and the ambiguities that result present formidable challenges to the viewer. The meaning of these images, and of much of Meatyard's work, is elusive. His photographs challenge us to find meaning not so much within the elements represented in the pictures, but rather in the responses that they evoke—responses that can be unsettling and even threatening. Accordingly, the challenges of the Lucybelle series are all the more apparent when we try to come to terms with the full scope of Meatyard's work—the "16 different styles throughout my photography." Much as Eugène Atget wanted to document all of old Paris, or August Sander wanted to photograph every German type, or Garry Winogrand wanted to photograph in order to see how the world looked when photographed, Meatyard turned his camera toward a wide range of subject matter, and it was this spirit of ongoing excavation—through lens, eye, and mind—that drove him. The diverse, sometimes uneven results of these excavations have confounded many critics and viewers ever since.

I believe that the main reason for Meatyard's relatively low profile is simply that his work is difficult to grasp, because of its complexity and its diversity. Neither condition is guaranteed to warm the hearts of viewers, curators, or critics. From beginning studio courses to high curatorial practice in major museums, a tangible sense of order and coherence is the major criterion for evaluating artists and their work, and this of course echoes our larger cultural preoccupation with order at any cost. Leo Castelli, the New York City gallery owner who for decades has been known for his ability to discover new and challenging talent, recently lamented:

> I never thought it would come to this. . . . I've always believed in development, one movement following another, the Cubists on the heels of the

Fauves, Minimal and Pop, and so forth. But everything today is very much in flux. There's so much happening now that it's difficult to sort things out.[38]

Alas, it has always been difficult to "sort out" any art worth considering. This craving for pigeonholing exists in many areas of our culture, but it is especially rife in the arts, with its various "schools" of art or literature, or "regionalist writers," or styles of jazz associated with St. Louis, Kansas City, or Chicago. It is important to emphasize, however, that such categories are almost universally denied and defied by the artists so labeled. They want to be taken on their own terms: warts, complexities, contradictions, and all.

LEXINGTON CONTEXTS

Like many photographers of my generation, my first extensive exposure to Meatyard's work came in 1974 with the publication of two posthumously published monographs, *The Family Album of Lucybelle Crater*[39] and the Aperture monograph *Ralph Eugene Meatyard*.[40] These two books hit a responsive chord immediately. Here was work that seemed to get at some of the spirit of the times in a fresh way. Meatyard's photographs of children and various props in decaying buildings had few antecedents, and they seemed to hone in on middle-class values with sharp, deadpan wit. If some of the pictures seemed like one-liners or hokey literary anecdotes, others swerved into unexplored mental territory. The picture of a young boy seated in the attic holding a small American flag (p. 162) seemed aimed directly at the generation that questioned the knee-jerk patriotism of "America: Love It or Leave It" bumper stickers. The multiple exposures, while fascinating formalistically, also served as reminders that we couldn't see William James's "big bloomin' buzzin' confusion" in the correct register, couldn't quite get a clear perspective on the thing itself. And the masked figures, with their twisted faces resting atop normal bodies set in everyday circumstances, were as freaky as anything in Haight-Ashbury or Greenwich Village. To my late-adolescent eyes, these images explored the contradictions that lurked beneath middle-class appearances. The photographs touched some of the same nerves as *Blow-Up, The Graduate, Catch-22*, or *The Crying of Lot 49*. An exhibition featuring Meatyard's and Arbus's photographs would result in a "family of man" very different from the one Edward Steichen envisioned in his 1955 exhibition, "The Family of Man," at The Museum of Modern Art in New York. Janis Joplin's scratchy blues and Charlie Mingus's throbbing bass would provide appropriate musical accompaniment.

If it was tempting in the early 1970s to view Meatyard's photographs from the perspective of the baby boomer, it is all the more tempting to do so now, with the aftermath of the Vietnam War and the powerful pull of nostalgia. Obviously, we are entitled to our responses, then and now. But the impulse to equate such interpretations with the *conscious intentions* of Ralph Eugene Meatyard should be severely qualified if not rejected altogether. Meatyard was, by virtually all accounts, a conservative, middle-class, Southern businessman. He had a difficult time coming to grips with the student unrest over Vietnam, and liberal friends remember long discussions about the war in which disagreements would flair up rather frequently. When one of his sons grew long hair, Meatyard's reaction was far from sanguine, and he had no sympathy for the drug culture. If some of his pictures look "stoned" or "spacey," it is not a reflection of the photographer's intentions.

Meatyard's work is devoid of political intent, even if some of his tableaux suggest the "generation gap" and the beleaguered nuclear family that were earmarks of the times. Meatyard was not a "concerned photographer" in the mold of Cartier-Bresson, Robert Capa, Werner Bischof, or W. Eugene Smith, who hoped that their photographs would reveal social injustices and effect change. Meatyard's aspirations lay in the timelessness of the mythic rather than the specifics of current social or political realities. His images dwelt more in the realm of inner consciousness than in the social or political fabric.

Like many twentieth-century artists, Meatyard kept his creative life quite separate from his business, and one of the most interesting challenges for those who study his life and work is to reconcile the apparent lack of connection between the outer appearances of Meatyard's everyday life and the states of mind and consciousness that fed his creativity. Meatyard read Wallace Stevens, T. S. Eliot, and William Carlos Williams with special attention, and he was doubtless struck by the disparities between the ordinary qualities of their daily lives and the extraordinary nature of their poetry. These poets, who, in the most creative periods of their lives worked as an insurance executive, a banker, and a physician, respectively, put to rest the myth that the artist must partake in the bohemianism often associated with the romantic notion of the *artiste*.

Working as an optician was not only a means of support for Meatyard but a source of genuine pleasure. He was proud of his reputation in the community as a fitter of eyeglasses, and almost two decades after his death customers remember his ability to fit glasses that rested perfectly on the face. He also enjoyed the social interaction with a wide range of people who frequented his shop. As they sat before him being fitted with new spectacles, some customers surely wondered about the avant-garde pictures that Meatyard hung on the walls of Eyeglasses of Kentucky. What did they make of these strange images? How might they have reconciled them with the conservative businessman who so ably fit them with spectacles? Meatyard's friend and fellow photographer Guy Mendes remembers that Meatyard "didn't seem nearly as unusual as his photographs. I think he was really distinctive in his pictures more so than in his personal self." [41] And Guy Davenport sums up the matter succinctly, "Meatyard lived an ordinary life, but he was far from an ordinary man." [42]

Meatyard lived in Kentucky throughout his photographic career, a fact that has filled some photographers and viewers with amazement. Seen from the perspective of New York, where much of the American art world was and is centered, Kentucky combines all of the elements of hinterland and backwater. Although many of our most notable creative personalities spring from intercoastal wastelands, the notion that art can only be made within the proper environmental seedbed—preferably New York or Paris—is still dominant and was exponentially more so in the mid-1950s when Gene Meatyard started taking photographs (when he wasn't fitting eyeglasses) in Lexington. More than a few commentators, then and now, are surprised to discover that a photographer in bluegrass environs somehow managed to make such strange and sophisticated photographs, and hardly a one with horses! They are even more astonished to hear that Meatyard apparently never *wanted* to be anywhere else or to escape to greener pastures: he traveled to New York only once, in 1967, and he never journeyed to the West Coast or Europe. He was quite content living in Lexington.

The fact that his friends in Kentucky included people of considerable gifts—Wendell Berry, Guy Davenport, Thomas Merton, and Van Deren Coke most prominent among them—explains to some degree Meatyard's lack of wanderlust. He was an insatiably curious man intellectually, but with such company his curiosity was more than amply satisfied. There were social gatherings and exhibitions at the forward-looking Lexington Camera Club, along with poetry readings and lectures at the University of Kentucky. Meatyard would occasionally travel to nearby Louisville or Cincinnati to hear lectures and meet photographers. And there were several collaborative projects.

Meatyard didn't meet Guy Davenport until the mid-1960s, when the latter joined the English Department at the University of Kentucky. When Davenport, a scholar with far-ranging interests, asked Meatyard to illustrate the cover of his book of poems, *Flowers and Leaves,* he was surprised that Meatyard insisted upon reading all of the poems in the manuscript before undertaking the photography. In these poems Davenport's erudition is in high fettle, in a manner reminiscent of T. S. Eliot and Ezra Pound, and Meatyard labored over the allusions, sometimes with a Greek dictionary at hand. The two had extensive conversations about the poems, with the result that Meatyard's copy of *Flowers and Leaves* became very heavily annotated. These efforts are suggestive both of Meatyard's intense intellectual curiosity and Davenport's influence upon him. Meatyard often spoke of the importance of bringing a "scholarly" perspective to his photographs, clearly having Davenport in mind. And when Meatyard would insist that photography's sister art was poetry, one could detect Davenport's influence, as well as that of Merton, Berry, and Jonathan Williams.

Meatyard's longest and most important collaborative project was with Wendell Berry. They worked together for two years on a book about Kentucky's Red River Gorge, a pristine forest east of Lexington. In the late 1960s and early 1970s, the Army Corps of Engineers wanted to dam the river, which would have destroyed the canyon. The gorge became a *cause célèbre* among environmentalists, who eventually prevailed in blocking the construction of the dam. Berry and Meatyard were in part politically inspired, but the project was also born out of their love for the countryside and one another's company. They spent untold days trekking and camping through the gorge area. Wendell Berry remembers one day during the collaboration:

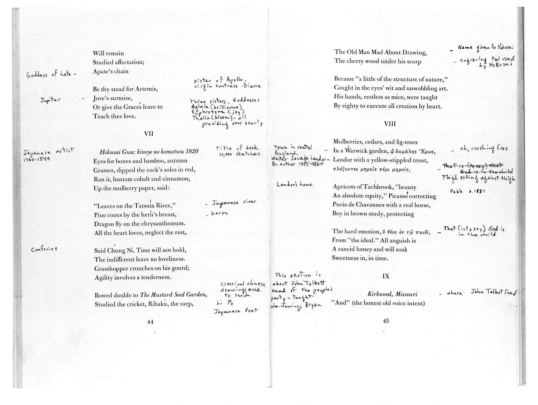

PAGES FROM GUY DAVENPORT'S POEM, *FLOWERS AND LEAVES*, WITH MEATYARD'S ANNOTATIONS

[We were looking for] something called the Indian Stairway, a bunch of hand holds in the rocks. Somebody had taken Gene and shown it to him, and we spent the whole afternoon looking for that stairway, and never did find it, and I never have found it yet. . . . We spent that whole afternoon going around and around through the woods looking for this, and, you know, cutting up and having a good time, and complaining, talking about it being hot, and telling jokes. I mean, it was the most undignified artistic collaboration ever carried out, I suspect.[43]

They exchanged prints and sections of Berry's manuscript, but there was little discussion between them about how specific images were chosen or how the book gradually took shape. Like so many artistic collaborations, the Red River Gorge project evolved more through intuition and silent rapport than through deliberative planning sessions.

Although Meatyard was surrounded by gifted and knowledgeable individuals who have since gained national and even international reputations, there was not what might be termed a "school" in Lexington. The talented men and women who lived in and around Lexington during the 1960s knew one another and one another's work, but their output reflects their own individual concerns. They saw each other sporadically, and then usually in social contexts that were not remembered for their philosophical discourse. They were all hard at work at their careers, and many, like Meatyard, had family responsibilities as well. Surely there was camaraderie, and surely they influenced one another, although, as is so often the case, the specific dynamics defy precise description.

The truth is that despite the considerable intellectual nourishment he got from the company he kept, Meatyard worked to a large degree in isolation, although he kept himself very well informed about developments in photography and the arts in general. As he wrote in a brief artist's statement for a 1961 exhibition at the University of Illinois: "Working in a fairly isolated area and feeding mostly on myself—I feel that I am a primitive photographer. I desire to make photographs that please myself. . . ."[44] Virtually every source we consulted and everyone we interviewed attested to Gene Meatyard's privateness. Berry, who spent considerable periods of time with Meatyard during their Red River Gorge collaboration, said he was a "very private kind of man. . . . [One] didn't know very much about Gene."[45] Jonathan Greene struck a similar chord, saying that "there are no keys—he's an enigmatic person. . . . The creative process was secret."[46] The words "enigma" and "mystery" often came up in the course of our conversations with Meatyard's friends. Those who knew him best freely owned up to the unknown sides of their friend Ralph Eugene Meatyard.

MENTAL CONTEXTS

The notebooks that Meatyard wrote during the late 1950s and early 1960s combined his own musings about photography with responses to a broad array of literary, aesthetic, and philosophical texts. He scored book margins with deep, heavy marks, sometimes adding lengthy comments or rebuttals. Meatyard displays in these entries a sharp critical intelligence. He was capable of reading like a scholar, carefully weighing and analyzing ideas. But more often he read with the eyes of an artist, gathering seeds anywhere he could find them.

His notebooks are filled with short, pithy sayings by diverse artists, photographers, poets, and philosophers. During the 1960s he copied short quotations on the envelopes of letters that he had received, including snippets from Henry Miller, T. S. Eliot, Thomas Pynchon, Edward Albee, Gertrude Stein, Albert Einstein, Paul Eluard, Richard Serra, Frederick Sommer, Arthur Rimbaud, Anaïs Nin, Ezra Pound, Beatrix Potter, Alexander Pope, James Agee, F. Scott Fitzgerald, Friedrich Nietzsche, Edgar Degas, Clement Greenberg, Minor White, Alfred Stieglitz, Voltaire, Suzanne Langer, Donald Justice, Allan Kaprow, Goethe, Lewis Mumford, Oscar Wilde, Willem de Kooning, Henrik Ibsen, Niels Bohr, Arthur Dove, and others. He sometimes added his own gnomic statements, as in the following reference (slightly misquoted) to Yeats's "Second Coming": "My pictures increasingly become more meaningful in a form of abstracted realism—what monster shambles forth to be born."

Meatyard tried to articulate and theorize his photographic practice in the late 1950s. Like many photographers of the period, he had discovered that there was precious little writing on photography that moved beyond the how-to banalities encountered in *Modern Photography* and *Popular Photography*. Serious photographers worked in a critical and theoretical vacuum.

Indeed, it was in part because of this vacuum that Ansel Adams, Minor White, Beaumont and Nancy Newhall, Dorothea Lange, and others founded *Aperture* in the early 1950s. Many of the photographers who gravitated toward this small-circulation but influential publication tried to develop a critical vocabulary that could bolster photography as a bona fide art and their own practice as worthy of serious attention. White, Smith, Meatyard, and others began casting their nets across disciplines in order to develop critical and theoretical concepts about their medium. They discovered that discourse born in other fields and concerns— aesthetics, poetics, religion, anthropology—often shed considerably more light upon the practice of photography than writings that purported to deal directly with the medium. In the late 1950s White, Henry Holmes Smith, and others attended workshops in which they tried to develop strategies for "reading" photographs by applying concepts developed by literary theorists like I. A. Richards. These early efforts to address problems of photographic representation, signification, and meaning appeared in the pages of *Aperture,* and though White and Smith soon called these experiments failures, they nonetheless had a significant impact upon younger photographers such as Meatyard. There were many issues embedded within these attempts at theory, but not the least of them was the need—shared by many visual artists across the ages—to put words on vision. Through discourse they could bolster and in some ways create their visual style.

Thus it is all the more interesting that by the early 1960s Meatyard had in large part stopped writing. The journals and notebooks of the late 1950s were abruptly discontinued after his heart attack in 1961, even though he continued his voluminous reading. When he did write or speak about his work he almost always discussed his pictures in formal terms, emphasizing shape, composition, the effects of light, and so on. Seldom did he broach the meaning of his sometimes astonishing images or acknowledge the dark side of his work. Meatyard's widow, Madelyn, recalls that in the privacy of their home he would talk in terms of the interplay of light and dark, shadows, and forms. The family would sometimes pore over abstract photographs such as the Light on Water series and discover anthropomorphic forms as music played in the background. She and their son Christopher remember how the music would open them up to seeing new things in an image upon repeated viewings.[47]

There is also consensus among Meatyard's friends about his pervasive silence on the meaning of his work. Photographer and friend Robert May remembers Meatyard talking about "what's on the surface rather than what was the hidden meaning, which I always admired him for, in that he left much for the beholder to carry."[48] Guy Mendes suggests:

> [Meatyard] learned from listening to others about his work. . . . I think Gene was eloquent in his pictures. Not that he spoke poorly or anything like that, but he just didn't speak that much about the content of his work or why he made these strange images. I think they were in there and had to get out.[49]

Bonnie Jean Cox recalls:

> [Meatyard] would bring over . . . a stack of newly mounted photographs, and he would just sit there like a teetotum, and watch your response, and there was never "yes, that's right" or "no, that's wrong, how could you think that that's what this photograph is about." It was always just sort of a sounding board sort of thing.[50]

And Guy Davenport remembers:

> Photographs were handed around. We saw the new pictures as they were printed and mounted, always in complete silence from Gene. He never instructed one how to see, or how to interpret the pictures, or what he might have intended.[51]

Other friends have agreed that Meatyard awaited their responses with eagerness.

There are various ways to explain Meatyard's pervasive silence. As he developed his distinctive vision in the early 1960s—one that centered around the images of his children with props and masks—perhaps the need for self-defining discourse diminished. Or he may have felt that the images lay beyond his powers of verbal articulation. And, too, he may not have known himself what some of his images meant or where they came from. When showing his prints Meatyard wanted to see what he could learn from the responses and remarks of a Davenport, Merton, or Berry, and he wanted to give them the freedom of following their own eyes and minds without prejudicing their responses. He may have felt that it was up to his viewers to close the circle that his pictures had opened. This was a familiar position in the late 1950s and 1960s, and many artists and writers adhere to it in our own time.

I am sure that many viewers of Meatyard's work will wonder, "What in the world did he mean by this?" The question will originate out of genuine bewilderment, but the answer will not be found in the testimony of the artist. Meatyard's silence puts us in the same position as it put his friends: if we want to wrestle with and perhaps grasp the meaning of these photographs, we need to attend to our own responses instead of looking to Meatyard for explanations or answers. If meaning is to be found, the onus for finding it lies squarely upon us, the viewers.

Meatyard's silence was also a function of the powerful influence that Zen held over him. He wrote in 1961 that "an educated background of Zen influences all of my photographs,"[52] and he repeated the assertion the rest of his life. In 1956 Meatyard worked with Minor White at a workshop at Indiana University in which White showed him how Zen could be relevant to photographic production and reception. A decade later Meatyard was strongly influenced by Thomas Merton, who had studied Zen and Sufi. But Meatyard was drawn to Zen on his own, and his study of the subject might be the most important way to understand his consistent silence with regard to his photographs.

Like many Americans who became interested in Zen during the 1950s and 1960s, Meatyard read Suzuki's *Zen Buddhism* with great care from start to finish. We might infer some sources of Meatyard's silence from the following passages from Suzuki, all of which are heavily marked in Meatyard's hand.

Untitled [Portrait of Thomas Merton with bongos], 1968

The worst enemy of Zen experience, at least in the beginning, is the intellect, which consists and insists in discriminating subject from object. The discriminating intellect, therefore, must be cut short if Zen consciousness is to unfold itself, and the koan is constructed eminently to serve this end.[53]

Words are merely a vehicle on which the truth is carried. Not comprehending the meaning of the old master, they endeavor to find it in his words only, but they will find therein nothing to lay their hands on. The truth itself is beyond all description, as is affirmed by an ancient sage, but it is by words that the truth is manifested.[54]

But silence can also originate in deep spiritual wellsprings, as suggested by the following heavily marked passage near the conclusion of Suzuki's book:

When a feeling reaches its highest pitch we remain silent, because no words are adequate. Even seventeen syllables may be too many. In any event Japanese artists more or less influenced by the way of Zen tend to use the fewest words or strokes of brush to express their feelings. When they are too fully expressed, no room for suggestion is possible, and suggestibility is the secret of the Japanese arts.[55]

Meatyard triple underscored the words "suggestibility is the secret," and indeed it may be the key to understanding not only Meatyard's silence but some of the challenges that his photographs present as well.

Meatyard felt that Zen was at the center of much of his photographic practice. In a letter to Van Deren Coke in the early 1960s he claims:

What shows through and is graspable in the works of E. Weston, Stieglitz, Strand and your [Coke's] work is this one thing (this seeing with the third eye)—whether these men were aware of Zen or not, they were using it in their work. . . . It is true, you can't say what Zen is, I can only state that it gets results for everything that we do—even in this Western world. . . . Like Stieglitz says that he wants his pictures to look like snapshots, only to have something more—this is the way to work. I feel that the things which I am doing now with other forms which I have done are the truest answer for the best of me. The uncanny or surreal combined with the perfect background, the formal, the no-focus & Zen awareness can produce a photograph of simplicity, power, interest, and the intuitive realization on the part of the seer or viewer that he is seeing more than he realizes.[56]

Meatyard's photographs of twigs and branches are among his most elegant and evocative compositions. On the back of many of the mounts Meatyard wrote the letter Z, which undoubtedly stood for Zen. On the title page of another heavily annotated book from Meatyard's library, Blyth's *Zen in English Literature and Oriental Classics*, Meatyard wrote the following note:

I need to participate in all types of my pictures—this is *me*, this is what Zen is & does!! A Twig is a twig, but being photographed by spectation [sic] it *can* be Zen (but, need not be, if not done well)—being made by participation the twig is me, or Zen, or God or whatever it may be called!!! [Meatyard's underscoring][57]

These pictures are Zen koans: mysterious, open-ended sources for contemplation and meditation. Their impact and meaning may lie beyond the reach of language, though our desire and need to articulate our responses to them may persist. And as we try to say what may be unsayable, these pictures, like Keats's Grecian urn, can "tease us out of thought."

CONCLUSION

As always, the creative process remains mysterious, confounding friends, family, bystanders, and even the artist himself. Influential people like Coke, Davenport, Merton, and Berry had direct impact on Meatyard as did writers, artists, philosophers, and photographers. Perhaps Meatyard's own childhood, of which he seldom spoke, returned to him through some of his images of his children. And surely the complexities of the 1960s shaped his most mature photography. There is much in Meatyard's biography and photography that could be grist for Freudian or Jungian analysis, and very different insights might be reached were his life and work viewed from a feminist perspective. But in the end, I fear, we must resort to grand clichés about his creative behavior: that the artist mixes and matches from the womb of the world and his or her interactions with it; that how or whether a particular grain of insight or experience filters through consciousness and does or does not emerge as a part of a work of art is ultimately unanswerable. What made Meatyard Meatyard is as elusive, finally, as the question is when applied to any of us.

Meatyard himself may not have known what drove him, or what his work "meant." Or perhaps, following Archibald MacLeish's famous dictate that "a poem should not mean, but be," Meatyard chose not to provide verbal clues to his photographs. The often-heard refrain of artists—"let the images speak for me"—may in the end be the truest of statements. (For that matter, silence may also be the truest statement a critic can make in attending to his or her responses to images, however self-abnegating the implications.) Trying to articulate what it meant to make these images or where they came from is as hard as trying to understand and then say how they make us feel now, some twenty-five years after their making. In the presence of these photographs, we mount (and maybe surmount) the crest of our personal horizons in search of meaning.

Meatyard's strongest work raises age-old questions of life and death, apparent and submerged realities, and the psychic structures that mediate experience. Unlike Aeschylus and Sophocles, Meatyard didn't need to depict the lives of the high and mighty in order to enact the tragic: dime store masks, abandoned houses, his own backyard, and compliant models were all that he required. In the end, perhaps the best we can do is point, sometimes with trembling fingers, to that murky realm of consciousness that Meatyard's photographs reach: what another American original, Emily Dickinson, called "zero at the bone."

Untitled [Self-portrait in room wallpapered with newspapers], c. 1967–68

Van Deren Coke

Ralph Eugene Meatyard

Gene Meatyard was a multitrack photographer, working on as many as four or five themes at the same time. In this way, when he found it difficult to continue on one path, he could campaign in another direction. He made what he called "No-Focus" pictures, which were generally of people. They were meant to be seen without reference to any particular subject. He also did informal, environmental portraits of the Catholic writer Thomas Merton, the folk singer and composer John Jacob Niles, the Kentucky poet Wendell Berry, and a few other friends. His series of impressionistic landscapes called Motion-Sound are multiple exposures of a motif on a single piece of film. Some of his straightforward landscapes are of the beautiful Red River Gorge which runs through the Kentucky mountains. In addition, he made a series of photographs he termed "abstract" and another of masked people collectively titled the Lucybelle Crater series. I feel, however, that his most important and personal pictures are those he called "surreal" and "Zen."

Meatyard was a restless romantic. He was a picture maker, not a picture taker, a man who expanded the definition of "reality" as he probed the mind's moods. Only on a few occasions did he meet with well-known creative photographers. He sustained himself creatively for twenty years by teaching photography to a band of devoted followers and by his contact with creative minds like Thomas Merton, Guy Davenport, Louis Zukofsky, and Wendell Berry. They and others influenced his thinking, but intuition played a major role in shaping his work. Many of his pictures were intended to evoke meditation and a mood of withdrawal. Perhaps this was why he was drawn to Merton and was such an admirer of Ezra Pound's poetry. Their views of life, while quite different, were attuned to life's mysteries. It is the feeling of mystery and melancholy in Meatyard's work that I find most moving. He seems to have recorded a whole world through the cracked crystal of a nineteenth-century flowered paperweight. To engender this feeling he had a special way of suspending in semidarkness strange and rhythmic shapes that have a sonority more felt than seen. Although I knew him well for all of his creative life, only now do I feel I may have a clue as to what his photography meant to him. Even so, I cannot decode the iconography of his work. That is part of its appeal.

Meatyard led a decorous middle-class life in suburbia. When his sons were youngsters he was deeply involved with the Little League on many evenings, and six days a week was a hard-working businessman. Photography, at first unconsciously and later quite consciously, provided him with a means of becoming part of another world. As he became more sophisticated he gradually became a willing captive of his very fertile imagination. His involvement in photography led him to study art history, poetry, and literature. Whole walls of his home became lined with books. In them he found ideas that influenced the shape and content of his photographs. Ideas expressed in words meant more to him than pictures. In 1962 he wrote to me, "I have just reread all the back issues of *Aperture*—they are truly inspirational." He spoke often of how stirred he had been by Edward Weston's *Daybooks*. It was the words rather than the pictures that influenced him. Meatyard traveled little, but he came to know a good many people in various creative fields. Davenport, a member of the University of Kentucky English Department faculty in Lexington, introduced him to a number of poets. They responded to his work earlier than did most photographers. This may mean that the feeling of enigma his photographs evoke is closer to the sensibilities of literature in verse form than to an eye attuned primarily to visual qualities. There certainly is much in poetry and literature that is analogous to his way of seeing. This is especially true of his moody, gothic pictures that engage our sensibilities in a manner reminiscent of the poetry of Edgar Allan Poe and Arthur Rimbaud. In his imagery the imagination is liberated and directed toward a fanciful world.

His imagery is undoubtedly visionary, but takes place in settings that are realistic. Objects lose their innocence and take on not before known connotations. Distance comes at you and scatters into fragments. These fragments may have lasted only a quarter of a second or for years; yet his pictures seem divorced from a span of time just as time is often unmeasurable in a dream. What he did was force the unselective eye of his camera to create photographs that deal with the shadowy and sometimes grotesque imagery we all carry inside us. Seldom was he satisfied with his subjects as he found them. He manipulated and mingled a staged half-world of masks, props such as flags and artificial flowers, parts of dolls, and long-handled tools. These he combined with blurred people situated in abandoned houses with broken windows and peeling flowered wallpaper. He had the ability to make a highly implausible situation seem real. He created dreamstates that were intended to promote contemplation. His pictures are closer to disquieting reveries than nightmares.

Zen was one of his major interests as were the philosophies upon which many other religions are based. He made very few comments about his work but he did say of Zen, "It is true, I can't say what Zen is, I can only state that it gets results for everything we do—even in the Western world. It is philosophy, more than a religion and a thing to do more than to talk about. . . . The uncanny or surreal combined with the perfect background, the formal, the No-Focus and the Zen awareness can produce a photograph of simplicity, power, interest, and the intuitive realization on the part of the seer or viewer that he is seeing more than he realizes."

Meatyard's "Zen" pictures are dominated by allusions to death, loss of identity, and the many different masks we don in the course of a day. He wrote in his notebook Nietzsche's statement "Every profound spirit needs a mask." His pictures of masked people create the sense of adventure. The ingredients are all there to help us dream backwards or even forwards. He draws the curtain back on scenes that recall the pageantry of a class play we were left out of in the first grade, late night movies seen when we are only half awake, or moments of stark reality we thought had been dismissed from our minds. He pushes to an extreme the camera's ability to suspend time and capture the quality and uneasy dimensions of unbound "reality."

UNTITLED [Red River Gorge #21: fog on stream], c. 1967–71

Wendell Berry

Remembering Gene Meatyard

I remember how I first met Gene Meatyard. It must have been about 1966. Jonathan Williams was visiting the University of Kentucky. One night he showed his slides of artists and writers, and among these was one of the Lexington photographer Ralph Eugene Meatyard. As I was walking out of the theater with James Baker Hall, he said he wished he could get to know Gene Meatyard, and Gene, who happened to be walking in front of us, turned around and stuck out his hand.

Coincidental or serendipitous as that was, it was like Gene. When he turned around, obviously tickled to be so ready to hand when called for, to meet the offering of the moment, he was very much in character. If he had materialized within a puff of smoke, he would not have been altogether out of character.

I remember sitting with Gene and Guy Davenport at Guy's house one night while Gene dealt photographs out to us one at a time from a stack. I remember the impression his eyes made on me. They were brown, wide open, and quick, looking with a kind of instantaneous curiosity first at his pictures and then at us, as if to see in our eyes what we saw in his pictures. And I remember the way his fingertips glanced and grazed over the surfaces of the photographs before he handed them to us; it was a little as though he touched the images into existence at that moment.

Not long after we met, Gene and his wife, Madelyn, invited Jim Hall and me over to supper at their house. It was a house full of books, of pictures and other things visually interesting, and of two kinds of hospitality: Madelyn's that was bright and warm and anxiously generous, wanting you to be pleased and to be at home; and Gene's that was also friendly and generous, but cooler than Madelyn's, and *interested*. At home as everywhere, he was alert and curious. In his presence I always felt more visible than usual, aware that I was being seen in a way that was undoubtedly not the way I saw myself. And for a man always frankly and vividly present, Gene was unusually reticent; he was invariably kind, attentive, and courteous, but he didn't tell you much about himself. I'm amazed, and amused, now to realize how many important subjects there are that I don't know his thoughts about. I knew, for example, that he was not very comfortable with my opposition to the Vietnam War, but we never really talked about this. I knew of his discomfort, mainly, because he would hand on to me his friend Thomas Merton's mimeographed position papers on the war, always with some brief comment, not condemnatory, but setting himself apart from them.

Guy Davenport rightly suggests that Gene's insatiable reading of books was motivated by curiosity and by courtesy. He read (for example) any available telephone directory because he was curious; he took delight in the oddity of people's names. And he read (for example) Louis Zukofsky because he had *met* Zukofsky and he would have thought it ungenerous or impolite to know a writer whose work he did not read. One could not be around Gene for long without becoming aware of his reading, not because he talked much about books, but because books were always piled around him and he loved to show them to you. They were as heterogeneous a lot as you would have expected. On one afternoon when we were talking in his shop, I remember, he showed me his copies of Kathleen Raine's *Blake and Tradition,* a biography of Beatrix Potter, and Guy Davenport's *Flowers and Leaves* (fully annotated).

The first record that my wife, Tanya, and I have of the Meatyards' visits to our house is for February 11, 1968, though I think the visits may have started earlier. Anyhow, Gene and Madelyn came often, bringing their younger children, Melissa and Christopher, and good things to eat, and always a camera. They liked it here, and we liked having them. Usually they would come in time for dinner on Sundays. I would get back from some morning outing to see their car parked in the shade in front of the barn. We would eat, and then take a walk or drive. I remember a Fourth of July picnic in the woods. And during Gene's last summer, he and Chris and I spent a long Sunday morning on the river in the canoe.

I loved to walk with him in the fields and woods because he was always looking. To walk with somebody who sees nothing or who never ceases to talk about what he has in mind is like seeing the land go to waste. Walking with Gene, I knew that nothing was wasted, and I knew, moreover, that surprises were coming. Sooner or later he would stop and lean intently over the camera, moving it around, stepping this way and that like a stalker. And what he was seeing or inventing to see was never anything that I would have predicted. I watched him photograph as stealthily as a wildlife photographer some skeins of discarded plantbed canvas in a farm dump.

One winter afternoon when the sunlight was coming almost level across the ridges, we were on the top of an eastward-facing bluff in the woods. Gene had the camera on a low tripod, and he was leaning over, peering into it, and at the same time holding his opened hand in the air. I saw what he was doing but wasn't paying much attention, assuming that he was shading the lens.

After some time he looked at me and said, "Do you want to see what I'm seeing?"

I did, of course. I walked over and looked down into the camera at another world. What he was seeing was a patch of white lichen on the side of a large ash. The patch was in full sunlight, and Gene had placed the shadow of his hand precisely in the middle of it. Framed by the camera, this altogether accountable sight became altogether unaccountable. It was unearthly, seeming to remove the ordinary elements of the vision out of ordinary time.

In, I believe, 1967, Matthew Hodgson, then at the University Press of Kentucky, asked me if I would be interested in writing a book about the Red River Gorge, which was under threat of being dammed by the Army Corps of Engineers. I said I would, and I suggested that the book should include photographs by Gene. This was approved by the press, and Gene and I, separately or together, began making trips to the gorge.

Being with Gene in the gorge was like being with him anywhere else: it was a pleasure with surprises. He was a good, always interesting companion. And though he was never assertively—and perhaps not even consciously—a teacher, I took much instruction from his presence and from his photographs. Such things are hard to demonstrate, but I know that I learned about the gorge, and thought and wrote about it, under the influence of his way of seeing.

Gene was as surprising a hiker as he was a photographer. He had a weakness for shoes that hurt his feet, and his pack would be incredibly heavy, its weight not to be accounted for entirely by photographic equipment. This weight would remain a mystery, unacknowledged by him, until the first evening, when out of the bottom of his pack would come, first, far better (and heavier) food than hikers normally carry and, second, a generous supply of martinis in cans, most acceptable to Gene's guests at supper.

The biggest surprise, however, came when Gene and Chris and Pete Harrod and I walked, or rather waded, through the upper gorge of the Red. On that trip, one stays in the river because the river offers the best footing and the clearest way. And yet even the river is an obstacle course of deep holes and enormous boulders, requiring strenuous labor of a walker, especially of a walker who carries a heavy pack.

After we were well into our adventure, Pete and I noticed that from time to time Gene would stop and take a small white pill. Finally, we asked him about it, and he told us in a completely offhand way that the pills were for his heart; he had had a serious heart attack in 1961. This was news to us. Nobody said anything, but I remember that Pete and I looked at each other and smiled, both of us thinking the same question: How could you get a man out of this place who could not walk out?

Gene's ruling principle, as man and artist, I think, was to keep out of his own light. And one of his principles, as a man, was to keep quiet about his principles.

As I look now at his Red River photographs I am impressed as never before by their darkness. In some of the pictures this darkness is conventional enough. It is shadow thrown by light; we see the lighted tree or stone and we see its cast shadow. In other pictures the darkness is not shadow at all. It is the darkness that precedes light and somehow includes it; it is the darkness of elemental mystery, the original condition in which light occurs. We are asked to accept the dark as the only condition or way in which we can see the light. And we are asked, then, to see how joyous, subtle, strong, intimate, familiar, and lovely the things of light are. The darkness of these pictures is an imagined darkness; and this was a courageous imagining, for the darkness is made absolute in order to make visible the smallest lights, the least shinings and reflections. Sometimes the lights require hard looking to be seen.

After he became ill with cancer, Gene continued to come with his family to visit us on Sundays. He continued to come after he was unable to swallow food; he would sit in the living room while the rest of us ate dinner in the kitchen. And he never conceded by so much as a look that these circumstances were the least bit out of the ordinary. Though he was dying, what he was doing was living.

Sometime toward the end, Gene made three photographs of himself rising up and going away over the top of a grassy ridge. He never saw these pictures; they were developed after his death by his friend Bob May and shown not long afterward in an exhibit of his work at Doctor's Park in Lexington. I had not heard of them; I came upon them unexpectingly. And this was my last, and in a sense my fullest, encounter with Gene. These photographs were his elegy and farewell, and their impact was physical. They came down like a sudden handclap upon everything I knew of him and felt about him. They removed at a stroke my fear that Gene, in refusing any concessions to illness, had somehow been ignoring it. He had been going away from us as he now revealed himself to us: fully knowing, full in the light, though, as the near horizon showed, there would be an end of seeing.

Plates

UNTITLED [Boy in front of warehouse], 1954

UNTITLED [Georgetown series: four children], c. 1955–56

90

UNTITLED [Two men sleeping], c. 1956

91

UNTITLED [Boy with sign, "red"], c. 1955–56

UNTITLED [Man with open mouth], c. 1955–58

Untitled [Cemetery statue], c. 1959

94

CEMETERY #32 [Double portrait on gravestone], 1960

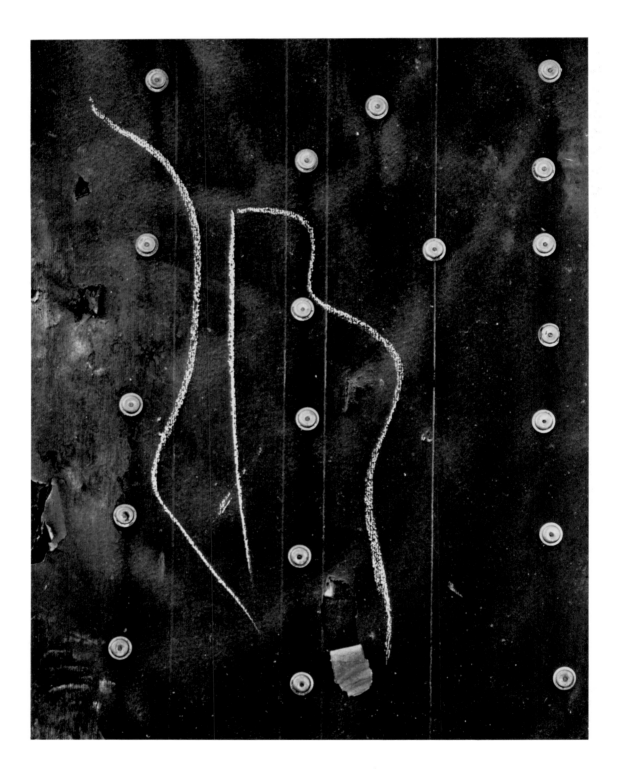

UNTITLED [Abstraction: chalk marks with nails], c. 1955–58

UNTITLED [Landscape: rock/face], 1960

Rock #3, c. 1957–60

GLASS, c. 1957–60

No-Focus #3 [Central form], 1959

UNTITLED [No-Focus: two figures against dark background], 1959

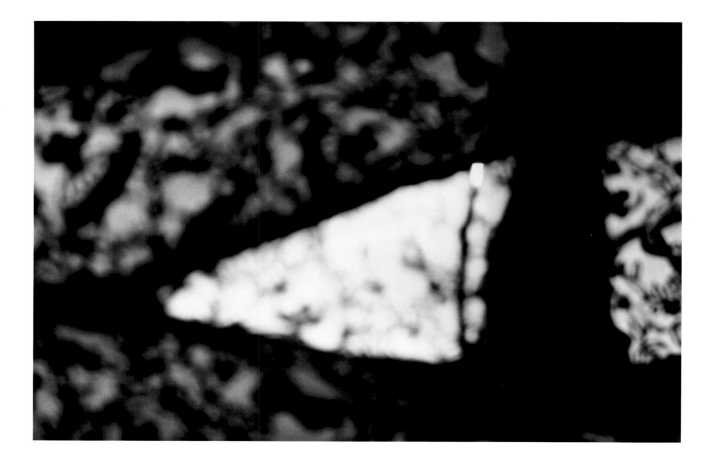

UNTITLED [No-Focus: triangle], c. 1957–58

Untitled [No-Focus: three figures with dark band on right edge], 1959

No-Focus #2 [Figures], 1960

Untitled [No-Focus: three figures], 1960

UNTITLED [Landscape: network of branches], 1964

UNTITLED [Light on Water], c. 1957–58

UNTITLED [Light on Water], 1959

Notes On The Keyboard Of The Imagination—#1 [Light on Water], 1962

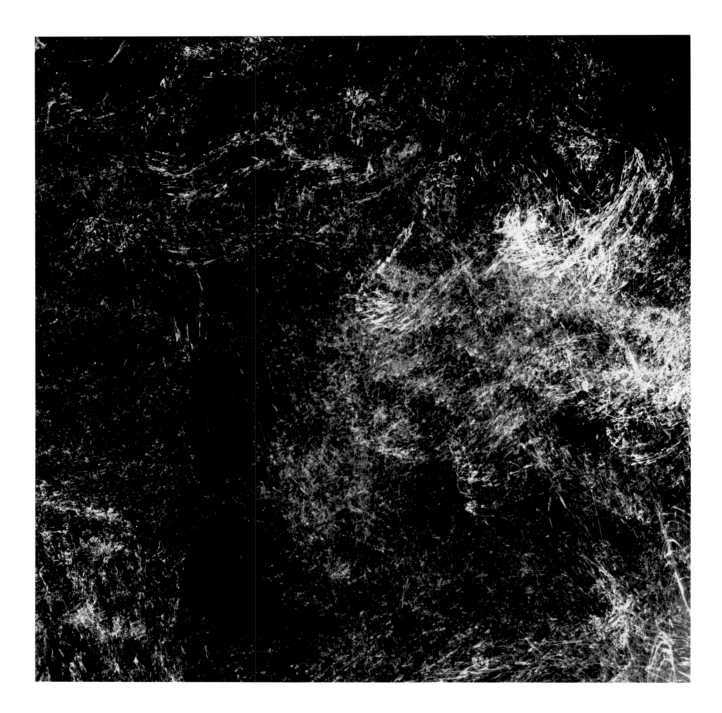

PORTRAIT OF SELF #6 [Light on Water], 1959

LITE #5 [Light on Water], 1959

Untitled [Light on Water: ideogram], 1960

UNTITLED [Landscape and sun reflection], 1963

UNTITLED [Landscape: pond with reflected branches], 1964

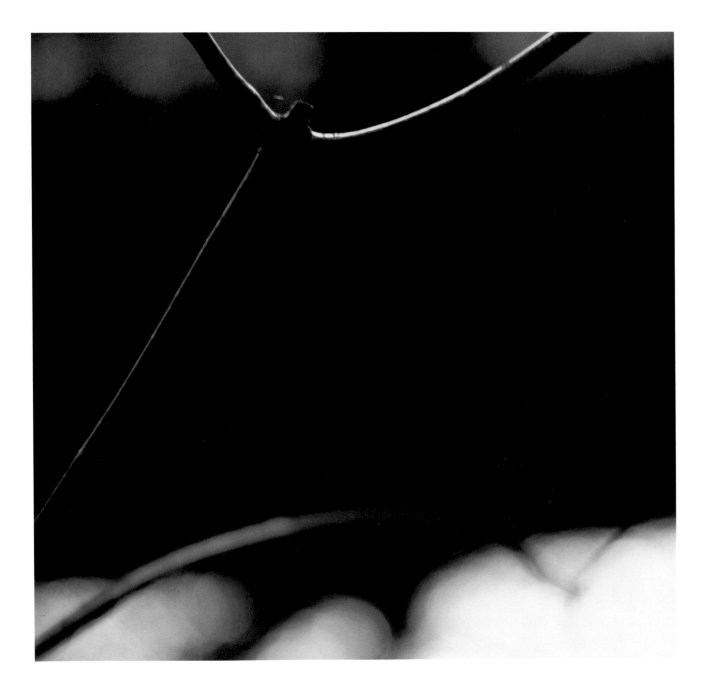

Untitled [Zen Twig], 1961

UNTITLED [Zen Twig], 1960

UNTITLED [Zen Twig], 1960

Untitled [Zen Twig], 1959

UNTITLED [Zen Twig], 1963

UNTITLED [Zen Twig], 1963

UNTITLED [Zen Twig], 1963

121

UNTITLED [Girl twirling in front of shed], 1965

UNTITLED [Two girls on porch swing], 1967

UNTITLED [Girl lying under tree], 1965

124

UNTITLED [Girl spread-eagled on rocks], 1963

UNTITLED [Boy holding mannequin hand], 1961

UNTITLED [Hooded boy by stream], 1963

Untitled [Blurred girl framed by chalk lines], 1963

Untitled [Two boys in door frames], 1960

Untitled [Two boys, one seen through hole in wall], 1962

Untitled [Interior with two boys], 1961

UNTITLED [Woman and child framing parallelogram window], c. 1970–72

UNTITLED [Girl atop woman], c. 1970–72

UNTITLED [Woman and girl waving in interior with chair], c. 1970–71

MADONNA, 1964

Untitled [Boy with pickax buried in wall], 1960

UNTITLED [Child with skull mask], c. 1962

Untitled [Boy below white mask and broken mirror], 1962

UNTITLED [Boy wearing white mask below broken mirror], 1962

UNTITLED [Masked adult with children in lap], 1962

Occasion for diriment [Young girl and masked boy beating his breast], 1962

UNTITLED [Boy with two masks climbing rocks], 1963

UNTITLED [Woman with mask in landscape], 1960s

UNTITLED [Group of children with dolls and masks], 1963

UNTITLED [Group of children with dolls, masks, and walking figure], 1963

Untitled [Interior with three children and three windows], c. 1964

Untitled [Interior with two figures, stairwell], c. 1970–72

To—El Mochuelo [Boys with noose], 1962

Untitled [Boy holding shard of glass before face], 1966

I Have Refused to Accept—#10 [Interior with hooded figure and shadow], 1966

UNTITLED [Child as a bird], c. 1960

Untitled [Masked woman with girl on ladder], c. 1970–72

Untitled [One-armed man with mannequin and mirror], c. 1958–62

Untitled [Male nude in bathroom], c. 1970

Untitled [Seated masked male nude], c. 1970

155

Untitled [Still life: gourd], 1964

Untitled [Still life: bird carcass on mirror], c. 1968–72

157

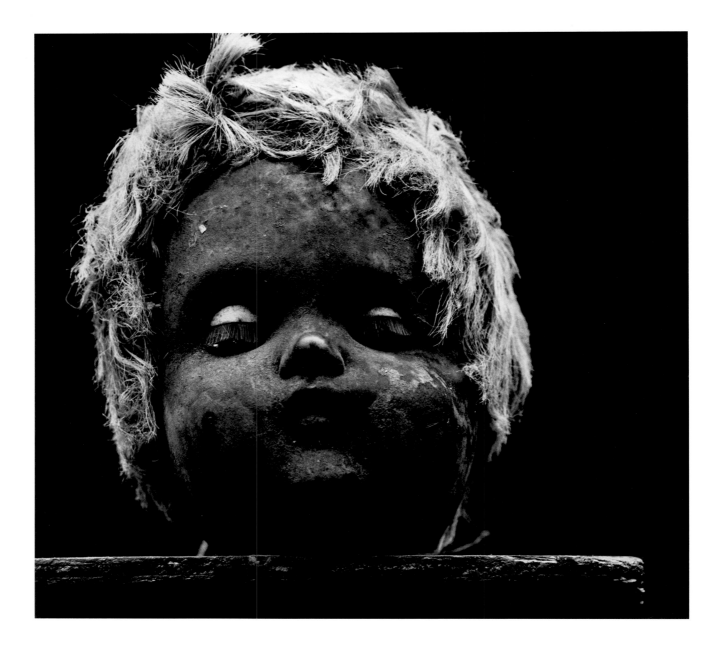

Untitled [Blond doll's head], 1959

UNTITLED [Brunette doll's head], 1959

UNTITLED [Still life: dolls and animals in glass jar], 1961

160

UNTITLED [Still life: doll atop photo], 1961

161

Untitled [Boy holding flag and doll], 1959

UNTITLED [Flag in water], c. 1970–72

UNTITLED [Motion-Sound: garden path with vortex], c. 1968–72

UNTITLED [Motion-Sound: forest], c. 1968–72

16—#8 MOTION [Motion-Sound: single tree], c. 1968–72

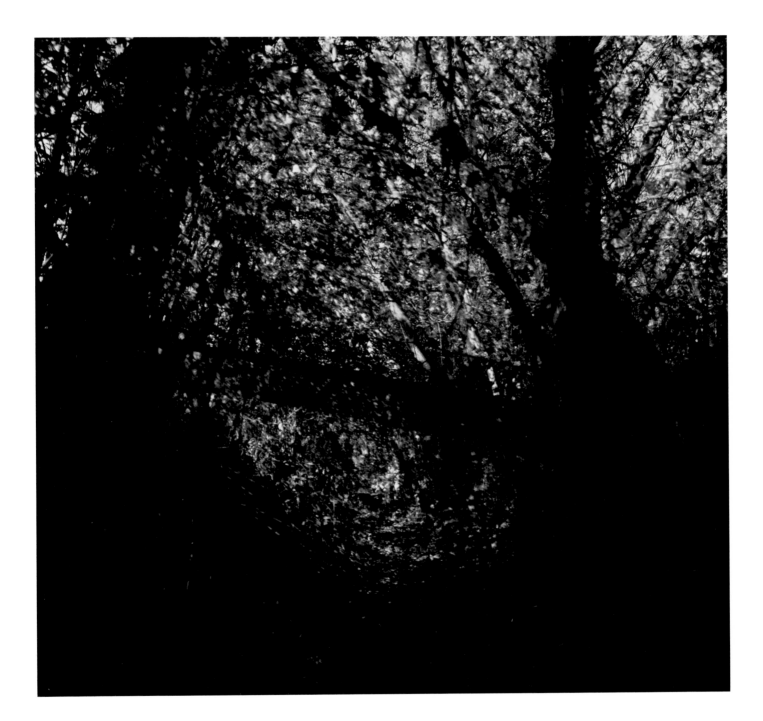

Untitled [Motion-Sound: abstracted tree], c. 1968–72

UNTITLED [Motion-Sound: building/mask], c. 1968–72

Untitled [Motion-Sound: urban building exterior], c. 1968–72

UNTITLED [Motion-Sound: façade with door], c. 1968–72

19—#11 Motion [Prone man on rocks], c. 1968–71

UNTITLED [Red River Gorge #1: Motion-Sound path], c. 1967–71

Untitled [Red River Gorge #16: log dam in stream], c. 1967–71

UNTITLED [Red River Gorge #48: inverted tree], c. 1967–71

UNTITLED [Red River Gorge #50: view through opening with light on leaves], c. 1967–71

Lucybelle Crater and her 40 yr old husband Lucybelle Crater

LUCYBELLE CRATER AND HER 40 YR OLD HUSBAND LUCYBELLE CRATER, c. 1969–71

LBC and Eastern man's friend, LBC, c. 1969–72

LUCYBELLE CRATER AND ONE OF HER GOOD MERTONIAN FRIEND'S SEVEN CHILDREN LUCYBELLE CRATER, c. 1969–72

Lucybelle Crater + 20 yr old son's 3 yr old son, also her 3 yr old grandson — lucybelle Crater

LUCYBELLE CRATER & 20 YR OLD SON'S 3 YR OLD SON, ALSO HER 3 YR OLD GRANDSON—LUCYBELLE CRATER, C. 1969–72

LUCYBELLE CRATER AND HER BEARDED BROTHER-IN-LAW LUCYBELLE CRATER, c. 1970

Lucybelle Crater + 20 yr old son's legless wife
Lucybelle Crater

LUCYBELLE CRATER & 20 YR OLD SON'S LEGLESS WIFE LUCYBELLE CRATER, c. 1969–72

Lucybelle Crater & 15 yr old son Lucybelle Crater

LUCYBELLE CRATER & 15 YR OLD SON LUCYBELLE CRATER, C. 1970

LUCYBELLE CRATER AND CLOSE FRIEND LUCYBELLE CRATER IN THE GRAPE ARBOR, 1971

List of Illustrations

The illustrations are listed below in chronological order rather than in the order of their appearance in the book. This provides an index through which to trace the development of Meatyard's work. All of the following works are included in the exhibition except those preceded by an asterisk, which are marginal illustrations for the essays. All photographs are gelatin silver prints and are in the possession of the Meatyard estate unless otherwise noted.

As Meatyard rarely titled his work, written identification of his images is confusing. Therefore, identification numbers for negatives, when available, are listed on the line below the title and date. Meatyard himself wrote some of these numbers on the back of the prints and mounts. His numbers usually include the year the photograph was shot. After the artist's death, all of his negatives were proofed. During this process, new numbers were assigned to the negatives. If two identification numbers are given for a print, the older number precedes the more recent one.

c. 1969
9–111–667
6 ¼ × 6 ¼ in. (15.9 × 15.9 cm)
Page 47

1969–71

LUCYBELLE CRATER AND HER 40 YR
OLD HUSBAND LUCYBELLE CRATER [Madelyn and Ralph Eugene Meatyard],
c. 1969–71
6–104–620
7 ⁷⁄₁₆ × 7 ½ in. (18.9 × 19.1 cm)
Page 176

1969–72

LBC AND EASTERN MAN'S FRIEND, LBC
[Van Deren Coke and Madelyn Meatyard], c. 1969–72
6–100–596
7 ⅜ × 7 ⁷⁄₁₆ in. (18.8 × 18.9 cm)
Page 177

LUCYBELLE CRATER AND ONE OF HER
GOOD MERTONIAN FRIEND'S SEVEN
CHILDREN LUCYBELLE CRATER [Madelyn Meatyard and Colleen O'Callaghan], c. 1969–72
6–97–583
7 ⁷⁄₁₆ × 7 ⁷⁄₁₆ in. (18.9 × 18.9 cm)
Page 178

LUCYBELLE CRATER & 20 YR OLD SON'S
LEGLESS WIFE LUCYBELLE CRATER [Madelyn and Candy Meatyard],
c. 1969–72
6–106–636
7 ⁷⁄₁₆ × 7 ½ in. (18.9 × 19.1 cm)
Page 181

LUCYBELLE CRATER AND 20 YR OLD
SON'S 3 YR OLD SON, ALSO HER 3 YR
OLD GRANDSON—LUCYBELLE CRATER
[Madelyn and Griff Meatyard],
c. 1969–72
6–106–633
7 ⁷⁄₁₆ × 7 ⁹⁄₁₆ in. (18.9 × 19.2 cm)
Page 179

1970

LUCYBELLE CRATER & 15 YR OLD SON
LUCYBELLE CRATER [Christopher and
Madelyn Meatyard], c. 1970
9A-6-66
7 ⅜ × 7 ⅝ in. (18.8 × 19.4 cm)
Page 182

LUCYBELLE CRATER AND HER BEARDED
BROTHER-IN-LAW LUCYBELLE CRATER
[Madelyn and Jerry Meatyard], c. 1970
6-100-598
7 ⅜ × 7 ⅜ in. (18.8 × 18.8 cm)
Page 180

UNTITLED [Male nude in bathroom],
c. 1970
9–116–697
11 ¹⁄₁₆ × 9 ¹⁄₁₆ in. (28.1 × 23 cm)
Page 154

UNTITLED [Seated masked male nude],
c. 1970
7 ¹¹⁄₁₆ × 7 ¾ in. (19.5 × 19.7 cm)
Page 155

1970–71

UNTITLED [Woman and girl waving in
interior with chair], c. 1970–71
6 ¾ × 6 ¹³⁄₁₆ in. (17.2 × 17.3 cm)
Page 134

1970–72

UNTITLED [Flag in water], c. 1970–72
8B-68 (224–227)
6 ⅞ × 6 ¹³⁄₁₆ in. (17.5 × 17.3 cm)
Page 163

UNTITLED [Girl atop woman],
c. 1970–72
6 ¾ × 6 ¹³⁄₁₆ in. (17.2 × 17.3 cm)
Page 133

UNTITLED [Interior with two figures,
stairwell], c. 1970–72
6 ¾ × 6 ⅞ in. (17.2 × 17.5 cm)
Page 147

UNTITLED [Masked woman with girl on
ladder], 1970–72
6 ¾ × 6 ⅞ in. (17.2 × 17.3 cm)
Page 152

UNTITLED [Woman and child framing
parallelogram window], c. 1970–72
6 ¾ × 6 ⅞ in. (17.1 × 17.5 cm)
Page 132

1971

LUCYBELLE CRATER AND CLOSE
FRIEND LUCYBELLE CRATER IN THE
GRAPE ARBOR [Madelyn and Ralph
Eugene Meatyard], 1971
6–101–603
7 ⅛ × 7 ⅜ in. (18.1 × 18.8 cm)
Page 183

1972

UNTITLED [Series of three self-portraits
with artist walking over hill], 1972
(Printed posthumously in 1986 by
Christopher Meatyard)
3 images, each 6 ¾ × 6 ⅞ in.
(17.2 × 17.5 cm)
Page 52

Untitled [Self-portrait as part of rebus of the artist's name], c. 1965–66

Chronology of the Artist's Life

1925

Born on May 25 in Normal, Illinois.

1943

Graduated from University High School, Illinois State University, Normal, and entered the navy. Attended Williams College in a predentistry program as part of the navy's V-12 program.

1944

Transferred by the navy to the hospital corps at Camp Perry, Virginia.

1946

Discharged from the navy, married Madelyn McKinney, and started apprenticeship as an optician in Chicago.

1949

Became a licensed optician and began working for the Gailey Eye Clinic, Bloomington, Illinois.

1950

First child, Michael, born. Left the clinic to enter Illinois Wesleyan University on the GI Bill. Attended for one semester and took a number of philosophy courses. Left school to work for Tinder-Krauss-Tinder, an optical firm in Lexington, Kentucky. Bought first camera (35 mm) to photograph his child.

1953–54

Isolated examples from this period include masks, fabricated scenes, use of the blurred image, and shots of his family in ruined buildings.

1954

Began serious study of photography. Took class with Van Deren Coke, joined Lexington Camera Club and the Photographic Society of America. Bought secondhand Leica. Exhibited nationally for the first time in group shows in Orlando, Florida, and Hartford, Connecticut.

1955

Second child, Christopher, born. Purchased a Rolleiflex (2¼ inch, square-format camera). Photographed cemetery headstones. With Van Deren Coke, documented the inhabitants of Georgetown Street, an African-American neighborhood in Lexington.

1956

Included in "Creative Photography," an exhibition organized by Van Deren Coke and shown at the University of Kentucky. Others in the show included Ansel Adams, Minor White, Aaron Siskind, Harry Callahan, and Edward Weston. Attended a summer photographic workshop at Indiana University taught by Henry Holmes Smith, Minor White, and Aaron Siskind. Introduced by White to Zen. Conducted a workshop for members of the Lexington Camera Club upon his return from Indiana, the first of many teaching experiences. Assumed a leadership role in the club when Van Deren Coke departed for Indiana University.

1957

First New York exhibition, a two-man show with Van Deren Coke at A Photographer's Gallery. Traveled to New York to attend opening. Made paintings inspired by abstract expressionism and "paintings in ice" (swirled paint and objects frozen in water in developing trays) which he then photographed in black and white; these projects continued into 1959. Resumed photographing cemeteries with series of funerary sculptures that continued into 1960. Photographed abstract patterning in textures of natural and man-made materials such as rocks, ice, mud, walls, and glass from 1957 through 1960. Started the Light on Water series, which he pursued throughout his career. Ended association with the Photographic Society of America.

1958

Disappointed after re-examining his previous work, did not photograph for three months, then began making No-Focus images shot with the camera out of focus. Began Zen Twigs series which continued through 1965. Placed various objects in jars and photographed them through the glass. Second trip to New York sometime between 1958 and 1960.

1959

Third child, Melissa, born. Had first one-person show, held at Tulane University in New Orleans. Portfolio of photographs and article by Coke appeared in *Aperture*. Included in show at The Museum of Modern Art, "Sense of Abstraction," organized by Nathan Lyons.

1960

Met poet, photographer, and publisher Jonathan Williams.

1961

Selected by Beaumont Newhall for inclusion in "New Talent U.S.A.: Photography" in *Art in America*. Had a heart attack and discovered he had suffered from gout for years. Was bedridden for six weeks and inactive for six months.

1963–64

Met Guy Davenport.

1965–66

Met Wendell Berry, James Baker Hall, and Jonathan Greene.

1967

Met Thomas Merton. Trip with family to Chicago, Rochester, Mystic Harbor, Boston, New Jersey, and New York. While in New York, met and photographed Parker Tyler and Louis Zukofsky. Opened own optical business, Eyeglasses of Kentucky, in Lexington. Began series of multiple exposures called Motion-Sound pictures which continued into 1972.

Late 1960s

Taught photography classes as part of the Free University of the University of Kentucky.

1967–70

Hiked, camped, and photographed in the Red River Gorge alone and with Wendell Berry in preparation for their collaborative book, *The Unforeseen Wilderness.*

1968

Organized "Photography 1968," an exhibition for Lexington Camera Club. Death of Thomas Merton.

1969

Began Lucybelle Crater pictures with book in mind.

1970

Gnomon Press monograph prepared and published by Jonathan Greene. Work began on a monograph edited for Aperture by James Baker Hall. Meatyard discovered that he had terminal cancer. Organized "Photography 1970" for Lexington Camera Club.

1971

Worked on organization of "Photography 1972" for the Lexington Camera Club.

1972

Died May 7 in his home in Lexington. Lexington Camera Club dissolves.

1974

Aperture monograph completed. Publication by Jonathan Williams and The Jargon Society of *The Family Album of Lucybelle Crater.* Limited edition portfolio of ten works published by the Center for Photographic Studies, Louisville.

1976

Retrospective exhibition organized by the Center for the Visual Arts Gallery, College of Fine Arts, Illinois State University, Normal (Meatyard's birthplace) and Independent Curators Incorporated. Tour included the American Cultural Center, Paris; this was Meatyard's first overseas solo show.

1977

Exhibition at Williams College Museum of Art, Williamstown, Massachusetts, "The Photographs of Ralph Eugene Meatyard."

1983

Exhibition, "Ralph Eugene Meatyard: Caught Moments—New Viewpoints," at the Olympus Gallery, London.

1991

New edition of *The Unforeseen Wilderness* released. Publication of *Father Louie: Photographs of Thomas Merton by Ralph Eugene Meatyard.*

Exhibition History

Compiled by Miriam Roberts and David Brown

1954

GROUP SHOWS

"Second Southeastern Salon of Photography," 1954 International Exhibition, Orlando, Florida.
"Seventh Hartford International Exhibition of Photography," Wadsworth Atheneum, Hartford, Connecticut.

1955

GROUP SHOWS

"Bergen County International Exhibition of Photography," Bergen County, New Jersey.
"Light and Shadow International," Rosicrucian Art Gallery, San Jose, California.
"Northwest International Photographic Salon," Puyallup, Washington.
"Seattle International Exhibition of Photography," Seattle Art Museum.

1956

ONE- AND TWO-PERSON SHOWS

A Photographer's Gallery, New York. With Van Deren Coke.

GROUP SHOWS

"Creative Photography," University of Kentucky Art Museum, Lexington. Invitational exhibition. Tom Maloney, in *U.S. Camera Annual,* 1957, refers to a national tour of this exhibition.
"1956 Exhibition of Photography by the Members of the Lexington Camera Club," Art Department, University of Kentucky, Lexington.

1957

GROUP SHOWS

"Exhibition of Photographs by Members of the Lexington Camera Club," University of Kentucky, Art Museum, Lexington, Kentucky.

1958

GROUP SHOWS

"Coke Collection," Indiana University, Bloomington, Indiana.
De Carava Gallery, New York.

1959

ONE- AND TWO-PERSON SHOWS

Tulane University, New Orleans.

GROUP SHOWS

"Art with a Camera," Louisville Arts Club, Kentucky.
"Photographer's Choice," Indiana University, Bloomington.
"Photography at Mid-Century: Tenth Anniversary Exhibition," George Eastman House, Rochester. Tour included M. H. De Young Memorial Museum, San Francisco, 1960, Wadsworth Atheneum, Hartford, Connecticut, 1960, and Museum of Fine Arts, Boston, 1961.
"Sense of Abstraction," Museum of Modern Art, New York.

1960

GROUP SHOWS

"Fotografi della Nuova Generazione," Milan and Pescara, Italy.

1961

ONE- AND TWO-PERSON SHOWS

University of Florida, Gainesville.

GROUP SHOWS

Arizona State University, Tempe, Arizona. Selections from the Coke Collection.
Morehead State College, Kentucky. With Drexel Wells and Cranston Ritchie.
"Photoshow," Arts in Louisville Gallery, Louisville.
"Seven Contemporary Photographers," George Eastman House, Rochester.
"Six Photographers," University of Illinois, Urbana.
"10th Boston Arts Festival," Boston.

1962

ONE- AND TWO-PERSON SHOWS

Carl Siembab Gallery, Boston.
University of Florida, Gainesville.

GROUP SHOWS

"Photography U.S.," de Cordova Museum, Lincoln, Massachusetts.
"Rhode Island Arts Festival."

1963

ONE- AND TWO-PERSON SHOWS

Arizona State University, Tempe.
University of Florida, Gainesville.

GROUP SHOWS

"Photography 63/An International Exhibition," George Eastman House, Rochester. Traveled to New York State Exposition, Syracuse; Institute of Design, Illinois Institute of Technology, Chicago; Indiana University, Bloomington; University of Illinois, Champaign-Urbana.

1964

ONE- AND TWO-PERSON SHOWS

El Mochuelo Gallery, Santa Barbara.

GROUP SHOWS

"30 Photographers," State University of New York at Buffalo.

1965

ONE- AND TWO-PERSON SHOWS

University of New Mexico, Albuquerque.

1966

ONE- AND TWO-PERSON SHOWS

Arizona State University, Tempe.

GROUP SHOWS

"American Photography: The Sixties," Sheldon Memorial Art Gallery, University of Nebraska, Lincoln.

1967

ONE- AND TWO-PERSON SHOWS
Bellarmine College, Louisville.
University of New Mexico, Albuquerque.
J. B. Speed Art Museum, Louisville, Kentucky. With Walt Lowe.

GROUP SHOWS
"Photography in the Twentieth Century." Traveling exhibition organized by George Eastman House for National Gallery of Canada. Tour under auspices of the National Gallery of Canada—1967: National Gallery of Canada, Ottawa, Ontario; Mendel Gallery, Saskatoon, Saskatchewan; University of Sherbrooke, Sherbrooke, Quebec; Winnepeg Art Gallery, Winnepeg, Manitoba; St. Catharines and District Art Council, St. Catharines, Ontario. 1968: Musée d'Art Contemporain, Montreal, Quebec. Tour under auspices of the George Eastman House—1968: University of California, Davis; Humboldt State College, Arcata, California; Baltimore Museum of Art; South Bend Art Center, Indiana. 1969: Civic Center Museum, Philadelphia; South Dakota State University, Brookings; Edmonton Art Gallery, Alberta, Canada; University of Kentucky, Lexington. 1970: State University of New York, Brockton.
"Photography International," San Jose State College, San Jose, California.

1968

ONE- AND TWO-PERSON SHOWS
Doctor's Park, Lexington, Kentucky, office building display area.
Quivira Gallery, Corrales, New Mexico. With Van Deren Coke.

GROUP SHOWS
"Contemporary Photographs," University of California, Los Angeles.
"Five Photographers," Sheldon Memorial Art Gallery, University of Nebraska, Lincoln.
"Photography 1968," Morlan Gallery, Transylvania College, Lexington, Kentucky.

"Light[7]," Hayden Gallery, Massachusetts Institute of Technology, Cambridge.

1969

GROUP SHOWS
"Photographs from the Coke Collection," Albuquerque Museum.
"Recent Acquisitions," Pasadena Art Museum, California.
"The Camera and the Human Façade," National Museum of American History, Smithsonian Institution, Washington, D.C.

1970

ONE- AND TWO-PERSON SHOWS
Institute of Design, Illinois Institute of Technology, Chicago. Selections from The Family Album of Lucybelle Crater series. Traveled to Creative Photography Gallery, Massachusetts Institute of Technology, Cambridge, in 1971.
Center for Photographic Studies, Louisville.
Ohio University, Athens. Photographs and assemblages.
Student Center Gallery, University of Kentucky, Lexington.
Visual Studies Workshop, Rochester. Traveling exhibition. Traveled to—1971: Jefferson Community College, Watertown, New York. 1973: Art Academy of Cincinnati; University of Delaware, Newark. 1974: Oakton Community College, Morton Grove, Illinois; Colorado Springs Fine Arts Center; Koeing Art Gallery, Seward, Nebraska. 1975: Kutztown State College, Pennsylvania; Millbrook School, Millbrook, New York; Elgin Community College, Illinois. 1976: The Linden Colleges, St. Charles, Missouri; Hartnell College, Salinas, California. 1977: Edna Carsten Gallery, University of Wisconsin, Stevens Point; University of Akron, Ohio; Norlight Gallery, Arizona State University, Tempe; Denver Art Museum. 1979: Youngstown State University, Ohio; Conkling Gallery, Mankato State University, Minnesota. 1980: Arkansas Union,

University of Arkansas, Fayetteville. 1989: Elvehijm Museum of Art, University of Wisconsin, Madison; Wyoming State University, Cheyenne. 1990: Johnson State College, Vermont; Pennsylvania School of Art and Design, Lancaster. 1991: Lowe Art Gallery, Syracuse University, New York; Joslyn Art Museum, Omaha, Nebraska. 1992: Hurst Art Gallery, St. Mary's Colleges, Monaga, California.
George Eastman House, Rochester.

GROUP SHOWS
"Photographs for Sale," Visual Studies Workshop, Rochester.
"Photography 1970," Morlan Gallery, Transylvania College, Lexington, Kentucky.
"Be-ing Without Clothes," Hayden Gallery, Massachusetts Institute of Technology, Cambridge.

1971

ONE- AND TWO-PERSON SHOWS
School of The Art Institute of Chicago Gallery.
J. B. Speed Art Museum, Louisville.
Picker Gallery, Dana Arts Center, Colgate University, Hamilton, New York.
Steinrock Gallery, Lexington, Kentucky.

GROUP SHOWS
"Photographs from the Coke Collection," Everson Museum of Art, Syracuse, New York.
"Lexington Camera Club 1971 Print Exhibition," Kentucky Educational Television Gallery, Lexington.

1972

ONE- AND TWO-PERSON SHOWS
Charles W. Bowers Memorial Museum, Santa Ana, California.
Columbia College Photography Gallery, Chicago. May have circulated.
Cortland Free Library, Cortland, New York.
Doctor's Park, Lexington, Kentucky, office building display area.
Focus Gallery, San Francisco.
Light Impressions, Rochester.

Logan Helm Woodford County Library, Versailles, Kentucky.
Matrix Gallery, Hartford.
Northeast Louisiana State College, Monroe.
Watson Gallery, Elmira College, Elmira, New York.

GROUP SHOWS
Florissant College, St. Louis.
"Photography '72," J. B. Speed Art Museum, Louisville.
"The Multiple Image," Creative Photography Gallery, Massachusetts Institute of Technology, Cambridge.

1973

ONE- AND TWO-PERSON SHOWS
Witkin Gallery, New York.

GROUP SHOWS
"1972–73 New Acquisitions," University of New Mexico, Albuquerque.

1974

ONE- AND TWO-PERSON SHOWS
Carl Siembab Gallery, Boston.
J. B. Speed Art Museum, Louisville. With Henry Holmes Smith.

GROUP SHOWS
"Photography in America," Whitney Museum of American Art, New York.

1975

ONE- AND TWO-PERSON SHOWS
Madison Art Center, Wisconson.

1976

ONE- AND TWO-PERSON SHOWS
Center for Visual Arts Gallery, Illinois State University, Normal. Organized by the Center for Visual Arts Gallery and Independent Curators Incorporated, Washington, D.C. Traveled to American Cultural Center, Paris; Leigh Yawkey Woodson Art Museum, Wausau, Wisconsin; and University Art Galleries, Santa Barbara, California; toured art centers of Kentucky; Ulrich Museum of Art, Wichita State University, Kansas; Wellesley College Museum, Massachusetts; and Oklahoma Art Center, Oklahoma City.

GROUP SHOWS
"Past into Present: Prints from the Monsen Collection of American Photography," Seattle Art Museum.
"Local Light: Photographs Made in Kentucky." Traveling exhibition organized by Guy Mendes and presented at Center for Photographic Studies, Louisville; University of Kentucky, Lexington; and other venues in Kentucky.

1977

ONE- AND TWO-PERSON SHOWS
Williams College Museum of Art, Williamstown, Massachusetts.
Western Carolina University, Cullowhee, North Carolina.

GROUP SHOWS
"Contemporary South." Toured the Far East and Europe under the auspices of the United States Information Agency.
"Photographs, 1977," Sheldon Memorial Art Gallery, University of Nebraska, Lincoln.
"The Grotesque in Photography," University of Bridgeport, Connecticut. Traveled to Neikrug Galleries, New York City.

1978

GROUP SHOWS
"'I Shall Save One Land Unvisited': Eleven Southern Photographers." Organized by Squires Art Gallery, Virginia Polytechnic Institute and State University, Blacksburg, Virginia. Opened at Corcoran Gallery of Art, Washington, D.C., then presented at Virginia Polytechnic Institute. Also traveled to Southeastern Center for Contemporary Art, Winston-Salem, North Carolina; Ackland Art Center, University of North Carolina, Chapel Hill; Greenville County Museum of Art, Greenville, South Carolina; Montgomery Museum of Fine Arts, Alabama; Cummer Gallery of Art, Jacksonville, Florida; Hunter Museum of Art, Chattanooga, Tennessee; High Museum of Art, Atlanta; International Center of Photography, New York; University of Kentucky Art Museum, Lexington;

University of Missouri, Kansas City; and University Museums, University of Mississippi, Oxford.

1979

ONE- AND TWO-PERSON SHOWS
Silver Image Gallery, Ohio State University, Columbus. With Eikoe Hosoe.

GROUP SHOWS
"Photographic Surrealism," New Gallery of Contemporary Art, Cleveland (now Cleveland Center for Contemporary Art). Traveled to Dayton Art Institute and The Brooklyn Museum.

1981

ONE- AND TWO-PERSON SHOWS
Yuen Lui Gallery, Seattle.

GROUP SHOWS
"Southern Eye, Southern Mind: A Photographic Inquiry." A joint project involving ten institutions. Meatyard's work appeared at University Gallery, Memphis State University.

1983

ONE- AND TWO-PERSON SHOWS
Olympus Gallery, London.
Prakapas Gallery, New York.

1984

GROUP SHOWS
"La photographie créative: Les collections de photographies contemporaines de la Bibliothèque nationale," Bibliothèque nationale, Paris.
"The Southern Tradition: Five Southern Photographers," Atlanta Gallery of Photography. The five photographers are Meatyard, Clarence John Laughlin, E. J. Bellocq, William Eggleston, and William Christenberry.
"Subjective Vision: The Lucinda W. Bunnen Collection of Photographs," High Museum of Art, Atlanta.

1985

GROUP SHOWS
"Images of Excellence," IBM Gallery of Science and Art, New York City.

Traveling exhibition organized by the International Museum of Photography at George Eastman House, Rochester. 1985: North Carolina Museum of Art, Raleigh. 1985–86: Norton Gallery, West Palm Beach, Florida. 1986: Santa Barbara Museum of Art, California; Cedar Rapids Museum of Art, Iowa; Landmarks Center, St. Paul, Minnesota; Toledo Museum of Art. 1987: International Museum of Photography at George Eastman House. Catalogue is titled *Masterpieces of Photography*.

"Celebrating Two Decades in Photography," Grunwald Center for the Graphic Arts, University of California, Los Angeles.

1986

GROUP SHOWS

"Théâtre des réalités," Metz pour la photographie, Metz, France. Traveled in 1989 to the Centre national de la photographie, Palais de Tokyo, Paris, as "Histoire de voir."

"Staging the Self: Self-Portrait Photography, 1840s–1980s," National Portrait Gallery, London.

"Photography: A Facet of Modernism," San Francisco Museum of Modern Art.

1987

ONE- AND TWO-PERSON SHOWS

Pace/MacGill Gallery, New York. With William Wegman.

Hewlett Gallery, Carnegie Mellon University, Pittsburgh.

GROUP SHOWS

"True Stories and Photofictions," Ffotogallery, Cardiff, Wales. Traveled to six venues in Wales.

"Modern Photography and Beyond," National Museum of Modern Art, Kyoto, Japan. Permanent collection show.

1988

ONE- AND TWO-PERSON SHOWS

"Southern Visions," San Francisco Museum of Modern Art. With Clarence John Laughlin.

Galerie Samuel Lallouz, Montreal, Canada. One-person exhibition in conjunction with a month-long photography festival "Le mois de la photo à Montréal."

GROUP SHOWS

"Vanishing Presence," Walker Art Center, Minneapolis. Traveled to Winnipeg Art Gallery, Winnipeg, Manitoba; Detroit Institute of Arts; High Museum of Art at Georgia-Pacific Center, Atlanta; Herbert F. Johnson Museum of Art, Cornell University, Ithaca, New York; and Virginia Museum of Fine Arts, Richmond.

1989

ONE- AND TWO-PERSON SHOWS

Tartt Gallery, Washington, D.C.

GROUP SHOWS

"Abstraction in Photography," Zabriskie Gallery, New York.

"The Lexington Camera Club 1939–1972," University of Kentucky Art Museum, Lexington.

"Evolving Abstractions in Photography," Anita Shapolsky Gallery, New York.

1990

ONE- AND TWO-PERSON SHOWS

Jan Kesner Gallery, Los Angeles.

Ehlers Caudill Gallery, Chicago. With Ruth Thorne-Thomsen.

GROUP SHOWS

"Photos de famille," La Villette (La Grande Halle), Paris.

1991

ONE- AND TWO-PERSON SHOWS

Comptoir de la photographie, Paris.

Bibliography

Compiled by Miriam Roberts and David Brown

MONOGRAPHS AND BOOKS OF PHOTOGRAPHS BY MEATYARD

Berry, Wendell, with photographs by Ralph Eugene Meatyard. *The Unforeseen Wilderness: An Essay on Kentucky's Red River Gorge.* Lexington, Kentucky: University of Kentucky Press, 1971. Reprinted by North Point Press, Berkeley, California, with a new foreword and revised text by Wendell Berry, 1991.

Coke, Van Deren. *Portfolio Three: Ralph Eugene Meatyard.* Louisville: Center for Photographic Studies, 1974. Limited edition portfolio of ten photographs with an introduction by Coke.

Greene, Jonathan, ed., with notes by Arnold Gassan and Wendell Berry. *Ralph Eugene Meatyard.* Lexington, Kentucky: Gnomon Press, 1970. Monograph.

Hall, James Baker, ed. "Ralph Eugene Meatyard," *Aperture* 18, nos. 3–4. Millerton, New York: Aperture, 1974. Selected photographs with a short foreword by Hall and "Reminiscences" by Guy Davenport. "Reminiscences" is reprinted as "Ralph Eugene Meatyard" in Guy Davenport, *The Geography of the Imagination,* Berkeley, North Point Press, 1981: 368.

Meatyard, Ralph Eugene. *The Family Album of Lucybelle Crater.* Millerton, New York: The Jargon Society, 1974. A fictional family album with texts by Jonathan Greene, Ronald Johnson, Ralph Eugene Meatyard, Guy Mendes, Thomas Meyer, and Jonathan Williams.

Meatyard, Ralph Eugene. *Father Louie: Photographs of Thomas Merton by Ralph Eugene Meatyard.* New York: Timken Publishers, 1991. Includes preface by Barry Magid, essay by Guy Davenport, correspondence between Meatyard and Merton, and reprint of Meatyard's eulogy for Merton.

CATALOGUES AND EXHIBITION-RELATED MATERIALS

A Photographer's Gallery. *Van Deren Coke/Eugene Meatyard.* New York: 1956. Exhibition announcement containing statements by the artists.

Bibliothèque nationale. *La photographie créative: Les collections de photographies contemporaines de la Bibliothèque nationale.* Paris: 1984. Text by Jean-Claude Lemagny.

Carl Siembab Gallery. *Photographs: Gene Meatyard.* Boston: 1962. Exhibition pamphlet containing artist's statement.

Colgate University, Picker Gallery, Dana Arts Center. *Ralph Eugene Meatyard.* Hamilton, New York: 1971. Exhibition handout.

Doctor's Park. *Ralph Eugene Meatyard.* Lexington, Kentucky: 1972. Gallery pamphlet with text by Jonathan Greene.

Ffotogallery. *True Stories and Photofictions.* Cardiff, Wales: 1987. Text by Susan Beardmore and A. D. Coleman.

George Eastman House. *Photography at Mid-Century: Tenth Anniversary Exhibition.* Rochester, New York: 1959. Introduction by Beaumont Newhall.

———. *Photography in the 20th Century.* Rochester, New York, 1967. Selections from the permanent collection, with text by Nathan Lyons. Catalogue for exhibition circulated in Canada by the National Gallery of Canada.

———. *Photography 63/An International Exhibition.* Rochester, New York: 1963.

High Museum of Art. *Subjective Vision: The Lucinda W. Bunnen Collection of Photographs.* Atlanta: 1983. Introduction by A. D. Coleman.

Illinois State University, Center for the Visual Arts Gallery, College of Fine Arts. *Ralph Eugene Meatyard: A Retrospective.* Normal, 1976. Essay by Van Deren Coke.

Indiana University, University Art Museum. *Photographer's Choice.* Bloomington: 1959. Exhibition catalogue with statement by the artist, contained in spring 1959 periodical of the same name.

International Museum of Photography at George Eastman House. *Masterpieces of Photography from the George Eastman House.* New York: Abbeville, 1985. Catalogue to the exhibition "Images of Excellence." Edited by Robert A. Sobieszek.

Lexington Camera Club. *Creative Photography 1956.* Lexington, Kentucky: 1956. Catalogue of the Lexington Camera Club invitational exhibition held at the University of Kentucky Fine Arts Gallery. Published as *University of Kentucky Art Bulletin* 1, January 1956. Text by Clinton Adams.

———. *1956 Exhibition of Photographs by the Members of the Lexington Camera Club,* Lexington, Kentucky: 1956. Pamphlet with short text by Meatyard.

———. *Exhibition of Photographs by Members of the Lexington Camera Club.* Lexington, Kentucky: 1957. No text.

———. *Photography 1968.* Lexington, Kentucky: 1968. Catalogue of the Lexington Camera Club exhibition held at Transylvania University, Morlan Gallery. Contains statement by the artist.

———. *Photography 1970.* Lexington, Kentucky: 1970. Catalogue for the Lexington Camera Club held at the Transylvania University, Morlan Gallery. Contains statement by the artist.

———. *Lexington Camera Club 1971 Print Exhibition.* Lexington, Kentucky: 1971. Catalogue.

———. *Photography '72.* Louisville: 1972. J. B. Speed Art Museum. Catalogue to exhibition organized by Meatyard, assisted by Robert C. May. Contains statement by the artist.

Meatyard, Christopher. "Endless Column: Retrospect for My Father R.E.M.," in *Le Mois de la photo à Montréal*: 1989. Produced by Vox Populi and edited by Nicole Gingras. Accompanied 1988 exhibition at Galerie Samuel Lallouz that was part of a month-long photography festival.

Memphis Academy of Arts. *Southern Eye, Southern Mind: A Photographic Inquiry,* Memphis, Tennessee: 1981. Now Memphis College of Art. Edited by Jack and Nancy Hurley. Contains texts by ten authors.

Metz pour la photographie. *Théâtre des réalités.* Metz, France: 1986. Published with the Centre national des arts plastiques, Fiacre. Essays by Philippe Lacoue-Labarthe, Patrick Roegiers, and Christopher Meatyard.

National Museum of Modern Art. *Modern Photography and Beyond.* Kyoto, Japan: 1987.

New Gallery of Contemporary Art. *Photographic Surrealism.* Cleveland: 1979. Text by Nancy Hall-Duncan.

Olympus Gallery. *Ralph Eugene Meatyard: Caught Moments—New Viewpoints.* London: 1983. Introduction by Martin Harrison and essay by Christopher and Diane Meatyard.

San Francisco Museum of Modern Art. *Photography: A Facet of Modernism.* New York: Hudson Hills Press,

in association with the San Francisco Museum of Modern Art, 1986. Photographs from the permanent collection with texts by Van Deren Coke and Diana C. du Pont.

Seattle Art Museum. *Past into Present: Prints from the Monsen Collection of American Photography.* Seattle: 1976. Introduction by Anita Ventura Mozley.

State University of New York at Buffalo. *30 Photographers.* Buffalo: 1964.

University of California at Los Angeles, Dickson Art Center. *Contemporary Photographs.* Los Angeles: 1968.

University of Illinois, College of Fine and Applied Arts. *Six Photographers.* Urbana: 1961. Contains statement by the artist.

University of Kentucky Art Museum. *Lexington Camera Club 1936–1972.* Lexington: 1989. Essay by Robert C. May, reprinted from an article by the same title in *Kentucky Review* 9, no. 2 (Summer 1989): 3.

University of Nebraska, Sheldon Memorial Art Gallery. *American Photography: The Sixties.* Lincoln: 1966.

———. *Five Photographers: Eikoh Hosoe, Ralph Eugene Meatyard, Josef Sudek, Garry Winogrand, John Wood.* Lincoln: 1968. Essay by Michael McLoughlin.

———. *Photographs, 1977.* Lincoln: 1977.

Whitney Museum of American Art. *Photography in America.* New York: Random House, Ridge Press, 1974. Edited by Robert Doty, with an introduction by Minor White.

Virginia Polytechnic Institute and State University. *"I Shall Save One Land Unvisited": Eleven Southern Photographers.* Blacksburg: 1978. Published by Gnomon Press, Frankfort, Kentucky. Texts by Ray Kass, James Baker Hall, and Jonathan Williams.

Walker Art Center and Rizzoli International Publications. *Vanishing Pres-*

ence. New York and Minneapolis: 1989. Foreword by Martin Friedman, with essays by Eugenia Parry-Janis, Max Kozloff, and Adam D. Weinberg.

Williams College Museum of Art. *The Photographs of Ralph Eugene Meatyard.* Williamstown, Massachusetts: 1977. Essay by Susan Dodge Peters.

BOOKS, ARTICLES, AND REVIEWS

Albright, Thomas. "Sinister, Surrealistic Art." *San Francisco Chronicle,* November 21, 1972: 43.

Anglin, Barbara. "Noted Photographers To Exhibit Works in Art Department March 26," *Rowan County News,* March 23, 1961: 6. Announcement of exhibition at Morehead State College.

Beaton, Cecil, and Gail Buckland. *The Magic Image: The Genius of Photography from 1839 to the Present Day.* Toronto: Little, Brown, 1975: 244. Biographical entry.

Block, Lou. "Meatyard Manifesto: The Coughing PSA." *Gazette of the Arts in Louisville* 1, no. 18 (June 1, 1959): 1.

Bloom, John. "Interview with Diana DuPont," *PhotoMetro* 6, no. 60 (June/July 1988): 21. Discussion of "Southern Visions" exhibition at the San Francisco Museum of Modern Art.

Bowman, Tom. "Death pervades exhibit," [Harrisburg, Pennsylvania] *Sunday Patriot News,* September 9, 1990: E2. Review of Visual Studies Workshop traveling exhibition at the Pennsylvania School of Art and Design.

Chiarenza, Carl. "Three Recent Shows at the Carl Siembab Gallery," *Contemporary Photographer* (Spring 1963): unpaginated.

Clarke, William Harry. "Meatyard Display," *Lexington* [Kentucky] *Herald,* February 4, 1968: 66. Regarding Doctor's Park Gallery exhibit.

"C. N." "Expositions," *Zoom* 44 (May/June 1977): 6. Review of the exhibition "Ralph Eugene Meatyard: A Retrospective" at the American Cultural Center, Paris.

Coke, Van Deren. "Creative Photography—1956," *Aperture* 4, no. 1 (1956): 4. Selected reproductions from the exhibition of the same title with brief biographies of the photographers.

———. "The Photographs of Eugene Meatyard," *Aperture 7,* no. 4 (Winter 1959): 154. Selected photographs and article.

Coleman, A. D. "From Dolls and Masks to Lynchings," *New York Times,* March 11, 1973: D26. Review of Witkin Gallery show.

———. *The Grotesque in Photography.* New York: Ridge Press and Summit Books, 1977.

———. "Latent Image," *Village Voice,* February 18, 1971: 16.

———. "The Directional Mode: Notes Toward a Definition" *Artforum* 15, no. 1 (September 1976): 55.

Contemporary Photographers, 2nd edition: 675. Naylor, Colin, ed. Chicago: St. James Press, 1988. Biographical entry by Jonathan Williams.

Crisler, Richard C. "Ralph Eugene Meatyard," *New Art Examiner* 17, no. 6 (February 1990): 47. Review of Tartt Gallery exhibition.

Davenport, Guy. "Ralph Eugene Meatyard," *The Geography of the Imagination,* Berkeley, North Point Press, 1981: 368. Originally published as "Reminiscences" in Hall, James Baker, ed. *Ralph Eugene Meatyard, Aperture* 18, nos. 3–4. Millerton, New York: Aperture, 1974: 127.

———. "Ralph Eugene Meatyard: Eight Photographs," *The Kentucky Review* 2, no. 1 (February 1968): text 33; photos in unpaginated insert.

Davis, Douglas. "Photography as Culture," *Art Culture: Essays on the Post-Modern, 70.* New York: Harper and Row, 1977.

Dean, Nicholas. "Meatyard Solo," November 1962. Boston newspaper review of Meatyard show at Carl Siembab Gallery.

Deschin, Jacob. "Two-Man Exhibition: Photographs of Teacher and Student Compared," *New York Times,* January 6, 1957: sec. 5, p. 18. Review of A Photographer's Gallery exhibition.

———. "Two at the Witkin, March 15 to April 8" *The Photo Reporter* 3, no. 3 (March 1973): 11. Brief announcement of exhibition at Witkin Gallery.

Ellis, Ainslie. "Notebook," *The British Journal of Photography,* April 15, 1983: 392.

Encyclopédie internationale des photographes de 1839 à nos jours/Photographers Encyclopedia International from 1839 to the Present. Auer, Michele and Michel, eds. Hermance, Switzerland: Editions Camera Obscura, 1985: unpaginated, two volumes. Biographical entry.

Gassan, Arnold. "Introduction to Photographs by Ralph Eugene Meatyard," unpublished manuscript, 1969.

Gilfoil, Brett. "Meatyard and Laughlin's Photographs of a Crumbled Freakish South at SFMMA," *The California Aggie,* May 25, 1988: "Art Think" supplement, p. 1. Review of "Southern Visions" in University of California at Davis student newspaper.

Glauber, Robert H. "Report from New York," *Skyline,* October 11, 1972: 4. Notice of Columbia College's Photography Gallery show, Chicago.

Green, Jonathan. *American Photography: A Critical History 1945 to the Present.* New York: Harry N. Abrams, 1984.

Gruber, Renate and others. *The Imaginary Photo Museum.* New York: Harmony Books, 1982. Contains 457 photographs from 1836 to the present with texts by Helmut Gernsheim, L. Fritz Gruber, Beaumont Newhall, and Jeane von Oppenheim. English translation by Michael Rollof.

Haggerty, Gerard. "Meatyard's Peripheral Vision," *Artweek* 8, no. 35 (October 22, 1977): 11. Review of "Ralph Eugene Meatyard: A Retrospective," at University Art Galleries, University of California at Santa Barbara.

Hall, James Baker. *"The Unforeseen Wilderness," Big Rock Candy Mountain: Education and Consciousness.* Menlo Park, California: Portola Institute 2, no. 1 (1971): 52. Book review.

———. "Snaps: Ralph Eugene Meatyard," *blue-tail fly* (Lexington, Kentucky) 1, no. 2 (November 11, 1969): 8.

———. "The Strange New World of Ralph Eugene Meatyard," *Popular Photography* 65, no. 1 (July 1969): 120.

Hall, J. B., and Wendell Berry. "Photographs by Ralph Eugene Meatyard" *Creative Camera* (London) 118 (April 1974): 130. Selected reproductions with quotes from Hall and Perry.

Harrison, Martin. "Ralph Eugene Meatyard," *Creative Camera* (London) 219 (March 1983): 866.

Haworth-Booth, Mark. "Letter from London," *Aperture* 92 (Fall 1983): 2.

Hoy, Anne. *Fabrications: Staged, Altered and Appropriated Photographs.* New York: Abbeville Press, 1987.

Imrie, Tim. "Ralph Eugene Meatyard," *The British Journal of Photography,* July 1, 1983: 676. Interview with Christopher and Diane Meatyard.

International Center of Photography. *Encyclopedia of Photography,* 323. New York: Crown Publishers, 1984. Biographical entry.

Kenner, Hugh. "The Distance From Normal: Ralph Eugene Meatyard's American Gothic," *Art & Antiques,* February 1987: 100.

Kielkopf, Larry. "Meatyard's Photos are Hauntingly Personal," *The Kentucky Kernal,* October 23, 1970: 3.

Kozloff, Max. "Meatyard," *Artforum* 13, no. 3 (November 1974): 68. Article reprinted in Max Kozloff, *Photography and Fascination*, 108. Danbury, New Hampshire: Addison House, 1979.

Lansdell, Sarah. "Meatyard, Gaines and Langland Surface on Tide of Art Activity," *The Courier-Journal* (Louisville), October 18, 1970: F16.

————. "Seeing Wilderness on its Own Terms," *The Courier-Journal* (Louisville), June 13, 1971: D12. Review of *The Unforeseen Wilderness*.

Leighten, Patricia D. "Critical Attitudes Toward Overtly Manipulated Photography in the 20th Century," parts 1 & 2, *Art Journal* 37, nos. 2, 4 (Winter 1977/78 and Summer 1978): 133; 313. Meatyard discussion in part 2.

Lemagny, Jean-Claude, and André Rouillé, eds. *Histoire de la photographie*. Paris: Bordas, 1986. English edition: *A History of Photography*, 198. Cambridge University Press, 1987.

Lemagny, Jean-Claude. "Ralph Eugene Meatyard, américain solitaire: une exposition accompagnée d'un catalogue (London, 1983)," *Photographies*, April 1984: 114, English summary, p. 135. Review of "Caught Moments—New Viewpoints" at the Olympus Gallery, London.

Lowe, Walter, "Eulogy for Gene—May 9, 1972," *Image* 15, no. 2 (July 1972): 20. Short obituary in the journal of the International Museum of Photography at George Eastman House.

Lufkin, Liz. "Wild-Eyed Visions in Odd Settings," *San Francisco Chronicle*, June 5, 1988: 12–13. Review of the exhibition "Southern Visions" at the San Francisco Museum of Modern Art.

Lyons, Nathan. "Photography '63: The Younger Generation," *Art in America* 51, no. 6 (December 1963): 72. Selections from "Photography 63/An International Exhibition" at the George Eastman House.

———— *Aperture* 8, no. 2 (1960). Special issue in conjunction with the exhibition "A Sense of Abstraction" at The Museum of Modern Art, New York, with text and illustrations selected by Nathan Lyons.

Macmillan Biographical Encyclopedia of Photographic Artists and Innovators, 409. Browne, Turner, and Elaine Partnow, eds. New York: Macmillan, 1983.

Maddox, Jerald C. *The Pioneering Image: Celebrating 150 Years · of American Photography*. New York: Universe Books, 1989.

Maloney, Tom, ed. "Creative Photography" *U.S. Camera Annual* 1957: 134. Selections from the exhibition "Creative Photography 1956," with text by Tom Maloney. Contains statement by the artist.

Marable, Darwin. "Confronting the Mask," *Artweek* 19, no. 21 (May 28, 1988): 11. Review of exhibition "Southern Visions" at San Francisco Museum of Modern Art.

May, Robert C. "Lexington Camera Club 1936–1972," *Kentucky Review* 9 no. 2 (Summer 1989): 3. Reprinted as essay in catalogue to exhibition of the same title, University of Kentucky Art Museum, Lexington, 1989.

Meatyard, Christopher. "Meatyard: The Last Self-Portraits," *Photographies*, April 1984: 115 and 135.

————. "Merton's 'Zen Camera' and Contemplative Photography," *The Kentucky Review* 8, no. 2 (Summer 1987): 122.

————. "The Wall-Mask Sequence of Ralph Eugene Meatyard," unpublished manuscript, 1987.

Meatyard, Ralph Eugene. "Remembering F. v. d. C." *The Kentucky Review* 2., no. 3 (Autumn 1968): 49.

————. "Thomas Merton Eulogized: 'Very Much With World.'" *The Kentucky Kernel*, December 13, 1968: 2.

"Meatyard at Steinrock," *The Courier-Journal* (Louisville), August 29, 1971: E7. Short item.

"Meatyard in Louisville," *The Courier-Journal* (Louisville), September 27, 1970: E7. Short item.

"Meatyard is the Rebel Leader," *The Courier-Journal Magazine* (Louisville), February 1, 1959: 18.

"Meatyard Photographs," *The Courier-Journal* (Louisville), June 4, 1972: E7. Short item.

"Meatyard Story, Prints Live Through Son," *Photogram* 1, no. 1 (March 1977): 2.

Mendes, Guy, ed. *Local Light: Photographs Made in Kentucky*. Lexington, Kentucky: Gnomon Press, 1976. Drawn from the traveling exhibition of the same name.

Murray, Joan. "Ralph Meatyard Photographs," *Artweek* 3, no. 40 (November 25, 1972): 9. Review of show at Focus Gallery.

Newhall, Beaumont. "New Talent U.S.A.: Photography," *Art in America* 49, no. 1 (1961): 52. Contains brief statement by the artist.

"Notes on Art and Artists," *The Courier-Journal* (Louisville), January 19, 1975: E7. Short item on postponement of exhibition.

"Openings This Week," *Courier-Journal* (Louisville), October 4, 1970: E7. Short item.

"Noted Photographer, 'Gene' Meatyard, Dies," *Courier-Journal* (Louisville), May 8, 1972: B20.

"Photographs from the 'Seven Contemporary Photographers' Exhibition, George Eastman House," *Contemporary Photographer* 2, no. 2 (Fall 1961): unpaginated. Contains a foreword by Beaumont Newhall and a brief statement by the artist.

"Portfolio: Ralph Eugene Meatyard," *Photo-World* 2, no. 3 (March 1974): 14.

Porter, Allan. "Ralph Eugene Meatyard," *Camera* (Lucerne, English edition) 53, no. 7 (July 1974): 24.

"Ralph Eugene Meatyard," *blue-tail fly* (Lexington, Kentucky) 1, no. 5 (February 1970): 15. Announcement of exhibition at Center for Photographic Studies and publication of Gnomon Press monograph.

"Ralph Eugene Meatyard," *Northwest Photography* 4, no. 6 (July 1981): 1. Review of exhibition at Yuen Lui Gallery.

Rannels, Edward W. "'Home Grown' Art and Photo Exhibit Now is Open at UK," *Lexington* [Kentucky] *Herald*, December 12, 1957: 6.

————. "Photography 1968 at Transylvania," *Lexington* [Kentucky] *Herald-Leader*, March 10, 1968: 52.

Rice, Shelley. "Dangling Conversation: Notes on Ralph Eugene Meatyard," *On Campus* (Garden City: New Jersey), October 1984: 25.

Riddle, Mason. "Vanishing Presence," *Arts Magazine* 64, no. 1 (September 1989): 80.

Rosenblum, Naomi. *A World History of Photography,* 571. New York: Abbeville Press, 1989.

Schikler, Jessica L. *An Annotated Checklist of Works By and About Ralph Eugene Meatyard,* unpublished thesis, University of Louisville, May 8, 1970.

Smith, K. T. "Photographer Catches Abstract," *Louisville* [Kentucky] *Times.*

Stitelman, Paul, "Notes on the Absorption of the Avant-Garde Into the Culture, *Arts Magazine* 47, no. 7 (May–June 1973): 56. Review of show at Witkin Gallery.

Tartarin, Michèle. "Meatyard: L'étrangeté révélée," *Clichés* (Paris) 25 (1986).

Tausk, Petr. *Geschichte der Fotografie im 20 Jahrhundert/Photography in the Twentieth Century,* 319. Cologne: Du Mont Buchverlag, 1977, and London: Focal Press, 1980.

Todd, Joyce. "Town Meets Gown," *Accent* (University of Kentucky) 1, no. 1 (October 1966): 12.

"Vanishing Presences: The Evanescent Moment," *The Journal of Art* 2, no. 1 (September/October 1989): 20. Review of the exhibition "Vanishing Presence" at The Detroit Institute of Arts.

Westerbeck, Colin L., Jr., "'I Shall Save One Land Unvisited': Eleven Southern Photographers," *Artforum* 20 no. 3 (November 1981): 83. Review of exhibition at the International Center of Photography, New York.

White, Minor. "Be-ing Without Clothes," *Aperture* 15, no. 3 (1970). Millerton, New York: Aperture, and Cambridge: Massachusetts Institute of Technology, Hayden Gallery, 1970. Special issue conceived and developed by Minor White in conjunction with an exhibiiton at M.I.T.

————. "'Light'": Photographs from an Exhibition on a Theme," *Aperture* 14, no. 1 (1968). Millerton, New York: Aperture, and Cambridge: Massachusetts Institute of Technology, Hayden Gallery, 1968. Special issue conceived and developed by Minor White in conjunction with the exhibition at M.I.T.

Witkin, Lee D. *A Ten Year Salute: The Witkin Gallery, 1969–1979,* 57. Danbury, New Hampshire: Addison House, 1979.

Witkin, Lee D. and Barbara. *The Photograph Collector's Guide,* 190, 288. Boston: New York Graphic Society, 1979.

Wright, George B. "A Vote of Confidence for Coke and Meatyard," *Village Voice*, January 30, 1957: 5. Review of exhibition at A Photographer's Gallery.

Lectures and Interviews

Interview of the artist by Nathalie Andrews in Lexington on February 25, 1970. University Archives and Records Center, University Libraries, University of Louisville, Kentucky: audio tape and transcript.

Lecture by the artist to the Midwest Society for Photographic Education, Louisville Conference, March 1972. Meatyard archives: audio tape.

Notes

FICTION AS A HIGHER TRUTH

1. Information in this essay is based on two groups of sources in addition to published material. The Meatyard archives, in the possession of the Meatyard estate, contains numerous papers, letters, and publications. David L. Jacobs and I interviewed many friends and family members of the artist, including Wendell and Tanya Berry, Bonnie Cox, Guy Davenport, Jonathan Greene, James Baker Hall, Robert C. May, Christopher and Diane Meatyard, Madelyn Meatyard, Melissa Meatyard, Guy Mendes, Thomas Meyer, Charles Traub, and Jonathan Williams. Descriptions of the optical shop's contents are drawn from interviews by the author with various friends of the artist, especially Guy Davenport (Lexington, April 25, 1990) and Guy Mendes (Woodford County, Kentucky, April 24, 1990, and Lexington, April 25, 1990).

2. Quotations introducing sections are copied from Meatyard's notes and diary.

3. Ralph Eugene Meatyard, interview with Nathalie Andrews, February 25, 1970, audio tape of transcript, University Archives and Records Center, University Libraries, University of Louisville, Kentucky.

4. Spelling of the family name varies with country of residence and time period. Sources for this information on the family background include Nathalie Andrews's interview (ibid.), discussions that David L. Jacobs and I had with Christopher and Diane Meatyard, and Nicholas Kilmer, *Thomas Buford Meteyard (1865–1928)* (New York: Berry-Hill Galleries, 1989).

5. Information on the Lexington Camera Club is derived from Robert C. May, *The Lexington Camera Club 1936–1972* (Lexington: University of Kentucky Art Museum, September 24–November 11, 1989). The text is a reprint of an article by May in *The Kentucky Review* 9 (Summer 1989) and from an interview by the author with May in Lexington on April 25, 1990.

6. Van Deren Coke, *Photographs 1956–1973* (Albuquerque: University of New Mexico Press, 1973) gives a chronology of Coke's life.

7. Information on Coke's class comes from copies of class handouts in the Meatyard archives; from May, *The Lexington Camera Club;* and from an interview with May by the author.

8. According to Christopher Meatyard, the 1955 cemetery pictures and the Georgetown series were taken with the 2 ¼ × 2 ¼ inch, square-format Rolleiflex that Meatyard had acquired the same year. He continued to use that format and make of camera throughout his career.

9. Meatyard's words are from a brief artist's statement that accompanied the exhibition "Pieces of Georgetown Street" when it was shown in Lexington soon after the series was completed. Meatyard archives. Coke's description was given during a telephone interview, January 12, 1991.

10. The Bauhaus was a German art and design school founded in 1919 and closed by the Nazis in 1933. In 1937 painter, sculptor, photographer, and theorist Laszlo Moholy-Nagy founded the New Bauhaus in Chicago with a number of other former Bauhaus faculty members. This school, which was soon renamed the School of Design and then the Institute of Design, was eventually incorporated into the Illinois Institute of Technology. Opposed to the distinctions between fine and applied art, both the New and the old Bauhaus had a rationalist and formalist approach, emphasizing problem solving and experimentation with materials and processes. Photography was deemed capable of expression as well as documentation and was thus awarded equal status with traditional fine art mediums. The Institute of Design Department of Photography has played a seminal role in modern American photography, either educating or employing a large proportion of the past half-century's most important photographers.

11. David L. Jacobs pointed out Smith's interest in the writings of I. A. Richards.

12. Information on the workshop is drawn from Henry Holmes Smith, "The Education of Picture Minded Photographers: A Symposium/Part 3," *Aperture* 5:1 (1957), 24–28; and from Meatyard's class notes, which are in the Meatyard archives.

13. Meatyard's teaching notes, dated August 9, 1956, and August 21, 1956. Meatyard archives.

14. Handouts were titled "The Control of Space," "What You Can Learn From Paintings," "The Shape of Your Picture," "The Effect of Abstract Shapes," "Dark and Light Values," and "Learning to See Creatively." Meatyard archives.

15. This appears to be the only diary Meatyard ever kept. Though fastidious in entering his progress and thoughts day by day, he abandoned it after a few months. In the typescript of his lecture to the Louisville Arts Club given on May 17, 1959 (Meatyard archives), Meatyard mentions the ice paintings and surface studies of ice, rocks, mud, and other substances, as still in progress. His brief venture into painting is especially interesting when compared with his sculptures, assemblages produced in the late 1960s. See note 77 for further information on the sculptures.

16. One painting on glass survives and is in the Meatyard archives along with the photograph made from it (see p. 22). One figurative painting and its photograph—a tonal and value study of a fish reminiscent of Bauhaus images and color exercises—are also in the archives.

17. January 2nd entry.

18. Volumes on art theory in his possession ranged from explorations of visual form by Rudolf Arnheim, Paul Klee, and Roger Fry to studies of the philosophy and uses of art by Ben Shahn, Suzanne Langer, John Dewey, George Santayana, José Ortega y Gasset, Marshall McLuhan, and Herbert Read. In addition to general histories of photography, Meatyard owned books on nineteenth-century figures such as Julia Margaret Cameron, George Barnard, Henry Peach Robinson, and Timothy O'Sullivan, and early twentieth-century photogra-

phers as diverse as Henri Lartigue, Lewis Hine, Henri Cartier-Bresson, E. J. Bellocq, André Kertesz, and Gyorgy Kepes. There are numerous catalogues and books of the work of contemporary figures. Once again, diverse viewpoints are represented, from those of Ansel Adams and Yousuf Karsh to Barbara Morgan and Imogen Cunningham, from Robert Frank and Danny Lyon to Frederick Sommer. Van Deren Coke, Edward Weston, and Harry Callahan are particularly well represented.

19. Guy Davenport, interview by the author, Lexington, April 25, 1990.

20. Ibid.

21. Those prints that have names—either written on the back or assigned to them in Meatyard's notebooks of work sent out for shows—are most often designated "Light" or "Lite" and followed by a number. In one diary entry (January 10), he referred to them as "fire" pictures. Meatyard did title several groups of the Light on Water images when they were sent out for exhibition. One he called *Portraits of Self*, another he titled with a quote from the medieval German mystic Meister Eckhardt, and a third was *Notes on the Keyboard of the Imagination*. It was sometimes Meatyard's practice to title an entire show with a single phrase, then identify the works within the exhibition by number. The same print sent to two shows could thus have different titles at different times. I am indebted to Christopher Meatyard for the description of these works as fire dancing on water.

22. According to his 1958 diary, Meatyard felt a strong affinity with the abstract surrealists, whose work also lends itself to this kind of subconscious suggestion. In the same entries, he also refers to the work of Morris Graves and of Stieglitz (presumably the Equivalents).

23. The individual images that are reversed are not identified by the artist. Christopher Meatyard feels that none of these images survive in print form.

24. These observations, made by Christopher Meatyard, are the result of his experiences in making contemporary prints from the original negatives.

25. Meatyard owned Kepes's *Language of Vision* (1951) and *The New Landscape in Art and Photography* (1956).

26. Examples of this work can be seen in Harry Callahan, *Photographs* (Santa Barbara: El Mochuelo Gallery, 1964), plates 89 and 90.

27. Callahan's images are all made with a tripod and a static camera: the movement seen is that of the water.

28. Meatyard described his working process in the Andrews interview.

29. This relationship is pointed out by Christopher Meatyard in an untitled, unpublished essay (Meatyard archives).

30. Ralph Eugene Meatyard, quoted in Beaumont Newhall, "New Talent U.S.A.: Photography," *Art in America* 49:1 (1961), 56.

31. Typescript of lecture given to the Louisville Art Club, May 17, 1959, Meatyard archives.

32. Ralph Eugene Meatyard, artist's statement in College of Fine and Applied Arts, University of Illinois, *Six Photographers* (Urbana, Illinois: University of Illinois, 1961), unpaginated.

33. Ralph Eugene Meatyard, letter to Henry Holmes Smith dated February 27, 1959. Meatyard archives. Holmes took this section of the letter and added it to an earlier statement from Meatyard to constitute the artist's statement for the catalogue of an exhibition, *Photographer's Choice* (Bloomington, Indiana: Indiana University, 1959), unpaginated.

34. Ibid.

35. Ibid.

36. Ralph Eugene Meatyard, "No-Focus," c. 1961, typescript of an unpublished essay, page 1, and Meatyard's lecture to the Louisville Arts Club. Meatyard archives. The above two sources, along with the artist's statement by Meatyard in *Photographer's Choice*, an exhibition catalogue, contain discussions of Meatyard's "discovery" of and work with No-Focus.

37. Ralph Eugene Meatyard, "Remembering F.v.d.C.," *The Kentucky Review* 2:3 (1968), 50.

38. Meatyard, *Photographer's Choice.*

39. Meatyard, "No-Focus," 2.

40. In order to retain the tones and shapes, Meatyard found that the No-Focus pictures had to be in focus in the enlarger. He accomplished this by focusing on the grain of the negative's emulsion. The artist explained his technique in "No-Focus" and Christopher Meatyard discusses it in his unpublished essay.

41. Though it is impossible to pinpoint, Meatyard's experience with delaying the development of the No-Focus works might have led him to apply this practice to all his work in the 1960s and 1970s. By that time, it was his habit to shoot during the spring, summer, and fall and to develop and print only during the winter. Having no permanent darkroom or printing setup in his home may also have contributed to that practice.

42. Meatyard, "No-Focus," 3.

43. One such image is *Eleanor and Barbara*, 1953, plate 26 in Callahan, *Photographs.*

44. Meatyard, "No-Focus," 4.

45. There is a single reference to a No-Focus image from 1961 in Meatyard's notebook that lists works sent out to exhibitions.

46. From notes in the Meatyard archives.

47. Drafts of correspondence in the Meatyard archives suggest that Meatyard did once write to correct a critic from whom he received what he felt to be an uninformed review, but Meatyard's friends and colleagues do not remember him contradicting their interpretations of his work.

48. Meatyard, "No-Focus," 4.

49. Paul Reps's compilation of Zen and pre-Zen writings, *Zen Twigs, Zen Bones,* (Rutland, Vermont, and Tokyo, Japan: Charles E. Tuttle Company, 1958) was in Meatyard's library.

50. Meatyard, "No-Focus," 3. He does not refer to these images by any name in the essay; instead they are just described as a body of new work.

51. According to his son Christopher, Meatyard may have used a macro lens or extension rings for increased magnification on some of these works in order to reduce depth of field and permit focusing on such a small area. Christopher Meatyard shared this information in conversations with the author and David Jacobs, Lexington, May 1990.

52. It is possible to give a precise date for most photographs that Meatyard produced between 1959 and 1967. The artist often wrote a negative number containing the year on the back of his works during that period. A few

works from the mid-1950s are also dated and several others can be pinpointed through references in publications and in the artist's notes and notebooks. Most dates for works before 1959 and after 1967 are approximate.

53. Van Deren Coke, "The Photographs of Eugene Meatyard, *Aperture* 7:4 (1959), 164.

54. Meatyard comments on his interest in Burchfield in both the 1958 diary and in a draft of a letter from around 1960 to Coke about the Zen photographs (Meatyard archives).

55. Coke, "The Photographs of Ralph Eugene Meatyard," 8.

56. Meatyard, letter to Coke, c. 1960.

57. Ibid. The Zen books were two of ten on a list from White that was probably handed out at the 1956 Indiana University workshop; their exact titles remain unknown.

58. Although Meatyard identified himself as Protestant when asked, he did not attend church regularly. Zen seems to have become his religion and his philosophy.

59. Meatyard, letter to Coke, c. 1960.

60. A book featuring these portraits of Merton has been produced: *Father Louis: Photographs of Thomas Merton by Ralph Eugene Meatyard*, edited by Barry Magid (New York: Timken Publishers, 1991). The postcards and notes that constituted the correspondence between the two men are reproduced in this book along with Meatyard's remembrances of Merton and an essay by Guy Davenport.

61. Meatyard, artist's statement in University of Illinois, *Six Photographers,* unpaginated.

62. Meatyard, letter to Coke, c. 1960.

63. Meatyard, "No-Focus," 4.

64. Guy Davenport and Bonnie Cox, interview by the author in Lexington, April 25, 1990.

65. Wendell and Tanya Berry, interview by the author and David Jacobs, Port Royal, Kentucky, June 3, 1990.

66. Andrews interview.

67. Meatyard shared his desire to convey sound and motion through still images with many painters that he admired including Wassily Kandinsky, the abstract expressionists, and American modernists such as Charles Burchfield.

68. Guy Davenport recalled discussing the cubists with Meatyard. Meatyard also owned a book that related cubism to the poetry of William Carlos Williams—one of Meatyard's favorite poets—and to the photography of Alfred Stieglitz—one of the photographers he felt had greatly influenced his own work.

69. Wendell Berry and Ralph Eugene Meatyard, *The Unforeseen Wilderness: An Essay on Kentucky's Red River Gorge* (Lexington, Kentucky: University of Kentucky Press, 1971), 31–34. The reproductions in the University of Kentucky edition are poor. The new edition published in 1991 by North Point Press has better quality reproductions and includes additional images shot for the project but not included in the earlier edition.

70. Part of a quotation by Cyril Connolly from Meatyard's notes.

71. Ralph Eugene Meatyard, manuscript of a prospectus for an exhibition to accompany publication of *The Unforeseen Wilderness.* Meatyard archives.

72. I am indebted to Charles Traub for this metaphor.

73. Berry and Meatyard, *The Unforeseen Wilderness*, 34.

74. Christopher Meatyard points this out in his essay, "Merton's 'Zen Camera' and Contemplative Photography," *The Kentucky Review* 7:2 (Summer 1987), 142, where he cites the above quotation from Thomas Merton, *Zen and the Birds of Appetite* (New York: New Directions, 1968), 34–35 and 46.

75. In his *American Photography: A Critical History* (New York: Harry N. Abrams, 1984), Jonathan Green finds a strong connection between the work of Diane Arbus, Meatyard, Bruce Davidson, Larry Clark, Max Waldman, Les Krims, Danny Lyon, and the rediscovered E. J. Bellocq, labelling them personal photojournalists. He argues that their approach was to assault the viewer visually and that their subject matter was emblematic of the obsessions of the time—the dangerous, the bizarre, and the unseemly.

76. Meatyard not only owned two versions of *Alice in Wonderland* but also a single volume containing Carroll's complete works.

77. Meatyard created a total of sixteen assemblages. Several are in the collection of the Walker Art Center, Minneapolis; the others are in the Meatyard estate.

78. Meatyard archives.

79. Meatyard describes the quotation's source as Marshall Berman, "On South Face," a review of Irving Gottman's *Relating in Public.*

80. Whitehall, the home of Cassius Clay, and Shaker Village, both near Lexington, have become important historic sites and tourist attractions.

81. Van Deren Coke, Introduction to *Ralph Eugene Meatyard: A Retrospective,* Center for the Visual Arts Gallery, College of Fine Arts, Illinois State University (Normal, Illinois: Illinois State University, 1976), unpaginated.

82. In a lecture Meatyard gave to the Midwest Society for Photographic Education conference in Louisville in March 1972, he said that the idea for the series came to him six years ago. A tape of the lecture is in the Meatyard archives.

83. May interview.

84. Meatyard, lecture to the Midwest Society for Photographic Education.

85. Some of Meatyard's images share a sense of the gothic and of macabre humor with the fiction of O'Connor and others classified as Southern gothic authors, but there is no evidence of any other direct use of such literature in Meatyard's work.

86. The book version of *The Family Album of Lucybelle Crater* (Millerton, New York: The Jargon Society, 1974) was issued posthumously, but Meatyard did work on the selection and sequencing of the images with the publishers. The volume includes captions for only the first and last images but does identify each of the sitters.

87. Gertrude Stein, *Lectures in America* (Boston: Beacon Press, 1935), 171. Meatyard, who owned the 1957 edition of this book, wrote a page in his notes on Stein's analysis of the relationship between description and emotion.

88. Jonathan Green suggests in *American Photography* that the Lucybelle Crater series is a 1960s version of Edward Steichen's famous 1955 exhibition at The Museum of Modern Art in New York, "The Family of Man." The exhibition included images of people of different personalities, occu-

pations, religions, races, and cultures, using them as generic examples to portray the universality of human experience. Steichen gave a rather rosy view of the world, implying that world peace and harmony should be attainable. Despite the highly personal nature of Meatyard's project, generalization of the specific is one of the major components of the Lucybelle Crater series as it was in "The Family of Man." However, Meatyard's images have a grotesqueness that belies Steichen's optimistic view of life.

89. A recent exhibition organized by Adam Weinberg explored the history of this type of image. Meatyard's work was featured prominently; in fact, one of his photographs was reproduced on the book's cover. Adam D. Weinberg, *Vanishing Presence* (Minneapolis and New York: Walker Art Center and Rizzoli International Publications, 1989).

SEEING THE UNSEEN, SAYING THE
UNSAYABLE

1. Wendell Berry, "Remembering Gene Meatyard," (p. 86 in the present volume).

2. Guy Davenport, interview with Barbara Tannenbaum, Lexington, April 25, 1990.

3. Ralph Eugene Meatyard, unpublished interview with Nathalie Andrews, February 25, 1970.

4. Ansel Adams, *Examples: The Making of 40 Photographs* (Boston: New York Graphic Society and Little Brown, 1983), 177.

5. Minor White, *Zone System Manual* (Hastings-on-Hudson, NY: Morgan and Morgan, 1968), 6. The technique is taken in more abstract directions in the 1976 publication of *The New Zone System Manual*, written by White and two collaborators. In that preface one encounters the following advice:

1. After grasping an intellectual meaning of some one zone . . . let your heart inform you about its emotional meaning. Still later let body-understanding inform you about the sensory nature of all ten zones, one at a time, as you feel ready.

2. When a formal, zone system meaning of the term "normal print"

has been digested, begin to ask how Normal relates to photograph's psychology; how it relates to an aesthetic sense, to your emotional experience of normalcy, and so on, seeing ever wider relationships.

6. Several of these photographers were included in Nathan Lyons's important exhibition, "Sense of Abstraction," which was shown at The Museum of Modern Art in 1959, and which contained Meatyard's work.

7. This project may have been inspired by Henry Holmes Smith, who would often insist that his students at Indiana University exhaustively photograph a section of the landscape or cityscape in order to determine what was actually there, as opposed to what the photographer thought was there, and therefore found. But then again, perhaps Smith got the idea from Meatyard and Coke, or maybe they all came upon it independently. All of this suggests the essential imponderability of issues of influence, and thus its considerable interest.

8. Jacob Deschin, "Two-Man Exhibition," *New York Times,* January 6, 1957.

9. Meatyard apparently only met Frederick Sommer once, after a lecture that Sommer delivered in Dayton, Ohio, in the late 1960s. James Baker Hall remembers that Meatyard was especially drawn to Sommer's work and had several reproductions of his images close at hand for many years. (James Baker Hall provided this information in an interview with Barbara Tannenbaum and the author in Lexington, May 1990).

10. Beaumont Newhall, "New Talent in Photography USA," *Art in America,* vol. 49, no. 1, (1961): 56.

11. James Baker Hall claims that Meatyard was an accomplished printer despite his unorthodox darkroom techniques. Hall and Richard Benson—both master printers in their own rights—once spent days printing Meatyard's negatives but failed to strike prints that were comparable to the originals. (This information was provided by James Baker Hall in an interview with Barbara Tannenbaum and the author in Lexington in May 1990.)

In correspondence with the author, Van Deren Coke suggested that some of the effects in Meatyard's prints resulted from the chloro-bromide pa-

per—Defender Velour Black—that Coke and Meatyard used at the time.

12. Group f/64 was an informal group of California photographers that included Edward Weston, Ansel Adams, Imogen Cunningham, Willard Van Dyke, and others. The name refers to a very small lens aperture that yields a high degree of sharpness throughout the picture plane.

13. At his death, Garry Winogrand, another passionate devotee of the process of camera-seeing, left 2,500 rolls of undeveloped film, along with 6,500 rolls that had been developed but never proofed, and an additional 3,000 rolls that had been developed and printed but only summarily edited. John Szarkowski, *Winogrand: Fragments from the Real World* (New York: The Museum of Modern Art, 1988), 35–36.

14. Ralph Eugene Meatyard, unpublished interview with Nathalie Andrews, February 25, 1970.

15. Ibid.

16. Ralph Eugene Meatyard, "No Focus," unpublished typed manuscript, unpaginated, c. 1961.

17. Beaumont Newhall, "New Talent in Photography USA," *Art in America,* vol. 49, no. 1, (1961): 52–57. The others photographers included in this article were J. Maund, Jr., Lyle Bonge, Don Worth, Richard M. Garrod, Ray K. Metzker, and Kenneth Van Sickle. Each was represented by a single image.

18. Beaumont Newhall, *The History of Photography* (New York: The Museum of Modern Art, 1964), 201.

19. It should be remembered that when *The Americans* appeared in the U.S. in 1958, it was greeted with very negative reviews, including one by Newhall.

20. For further discussion of this correspondence and its importance in mid-twentieth-century photography, see my "Labyrinths," *The Archive* (Center for Creative Photography, June 1986), 16–45 and "Frederick Sommer: A Portrait in Prisms," *Afterimage* (October 1988), 14–16.

21. In the 1982 edition of the *History,* Newhall had little choice but to include more work in this vein, since the images of Diane Arbus, Lee Friedlander, and Garry Winogrand could hardly be excluded. But the text and many of the images reproduced reveal

the same agendas that were at work in the earlier editions.

22. John Szarkowski, *Photography Until Now* (New York and Boston: The Museum of Modern Art and Little Brown, 1989).

23. Sarah Greenough et al., *On the Art of Fixing a Shadow* (Washington, D.C. and Chicago: National Gallery and The Art Institute of Chicago, 1989).

24. James Enyeart, ed., *Decade by Decade* (Tuscon, Arizona: Center for Creative Photography and Boston: Little Brown, 1989).

25. Adam D. Weinberg, *Vanishing Presence* (Minneapolis and New York: Walker Art Center, 1989, and Rizzoli International Publications).

26. Naomi Rosenblum reproduces a Meatyard photograph in *A World History of Photography* (New York: Abbeville, 1984, 572), and he is also included in Anne Hoy's *Fabrications: Staged, Altered and Appropriated Photographs* (New York: Abbeville, 1987). It is interesting that Meatyard's reputation is more established in Europe than in America, as witnessed not only by European exhibitions in recent years (see List of Exhibitions) but by his position in a book like Lemagny's and Rouillé's *A History of Photography* (Cambridge: Cambridge University Press, 1986).

27. Anne H. Hoy, *Fabrications: Staged, Altered and Appropriated Photographs*, 10.

28. Van Deren Coke, "The Photographs of Eugene Meatyard," *Aperture* 7:1, 1959, 156.

29. In a 1970 interview Meatyard discussed some benefits of delaying film processing and printing:

I'd shoot the whole [roll of film and] I'd put it away and I wouldn't do anything more with it for a year. . . . and so I got onto another thing which I did a whole lot of for a long time, and that was to not see my pictures for a long time so I wouldn't be biased toward them. Usually with anything that you create you'll make a thing and the last one you did is the best one you ever did. . . . something along that line, and after a little while you're cool towards it.

Ralph Eugene Meatyard, unpub-lished interview with Nathalie Andrews, February 25, 1970.

30. The nudes were photographed expressly for Minor White's exhibition and subsequent Aperture monograph, *Be-ing without Clothes.*

31. Ralph Eugene Meatyard, lecture delivered to the Midwestern Meeting of the Society for Photographic Education, Louisville, March 1972.

32. Ralph Eugene Meatyard, *Creative Photography 1956* (Lexington: Lexington Camera Club, 1956), 18. Quoted in Robert C. May, *The Lexington Camera Club, 1936–1972* (Lexington: University of Kentucky Art Museum, 1989), unpaginated.

33. Wendell Berry, "Remembering Gene Meatyard," p. 85 in the present volume.

34. On the last page of *The Family Album of Lucybelle Crater* (Millerton, New York: Jargon Press, 1974), Ralph Eugene Meatyard is identified as appearing only on the first plate, *Lucybelle Crater and her 46-year old husband Lucybelle Crater.* The final plate, in which Gene posed as Lucybelle and Madelyn as "her close friend Lucybelle Crater," was identified only as *Mystery People* in the appendix of the book.

35. Although several of the images were titled by Meatyard, only two of the pictures published in *The Family Album of Lucybelle Crater* bore titles in the book: the first and last pictures, which featured Gene and Madelyn Meatyard in reversed roles (see note 34). We should recall, however, that this book, as well as the Aperture monograph, were produced after Meatyard's death. The Lucybelle photographs included in the exhibition and book bear Meatyard's original titles.

36. The work of these three photographers was introduced to a national audience in John Szarkowski's exhibition, "New Documentary Photography" (Museum of Modern Art, 1967).

37. Gertrude Stein's famous if seldom understood statement about "a rose . . ." as well as Flannery O'Connor's sense of Gothic appearances vs. reality (Lucy Nell Crater is a character in O'Connor's story "The Life You Save May Be Your Own") were acknowledged influences for the Lucybelle series. In her accompanying essay, Barbara Tannenbaum talks at greater length about these influences.

38. Grace Glueck, "Leo Castelli Takes Stock of 30 Years of Selling Art," *New York Times,* February 5, 1987, p. 20.

39. Ralph Eugene Meatyard, *The Family Album of Lucybelle Crater.*

40. *Ralph Eugene Meatyard,* ed. James Baker Hall (*Aperture* 18:3&4, 1974).

41. Guy Mendes, interview with Barbara Tannenbaum, Lexington, April 24, 1990.

42. Guy Davenport and Bonnie Jean Cox, interview with Barbara Tannenbaum, Lexington, April 25, 1990.

43. Wendell Berry, interview with David L. Jacobs and Barbara Tannenbaum, at the Berrys' farm, Kentucky, June 1990.

44. Ralph Eugene Meatyard, "Personal Statement," *Six Photographers* (Urbana: University of Illinois, 1961), unpaginated.

45. Wendell Berry, interview with David L. Jacobs and Barbara Tannenbaum.

46. Jonathan Green, interview with David L. Jacobs and Barbara Tannenbaum, Lexington, June 1990.

47. Madelyn Meatyard, Christopher Meatyard, Melissa Meatyard, informal interview with David L. Jacobs and Barbara Tannenbaum, Lexington, May 1990.

48. Robert May, interview with Barbara Tannenbaum, Lexington, April 25, 1990.

49. Guy Mendes, interview with Barbara Tannenbaum, Lexington, April 24, 1990.

50. Guy Davenport and Bonnie Jean Cox, interview with Barbara Tannenbaum, Lexington, April 25, 1990.

51. Guy Davenport, "Ralph Eugene Meatyard," *The Geography of the Imagination* (San Francisco: North Point Press, 1981), 369.

52. Ralph Eugene Meatyard, "Personal Statement," *Six Photographers* (Urbana: University of Illinois, 1961), unpaginated.

53. D. T. Suzuki, *Zen Buddhism,* ed. William Barrett (Garden City, NY: Doubleday and Company, 1956), 137.

54. Ibid., 138.

55. Ibid., 287.

56. Ralph Eugene Meatyard, typed letter to Van Deren Coke (c. 1960). Meatyard archives.

57. R. H. Blyth, *Zen in English Literature and Oriental Classics* (New York: Dutton, 1960). This book was as systematically read as Suzuki's and especially so in the passages dealing with death, ambiguity, and paradox. On the title page, for example, Meatyard wrote:

> pictures of people [with] masks or as actors are examples of me playing *God!!*

> It is only through form that we can realize emptiness!

> Beyond this place, there be dragons—from Medieval maps

Akron Art Museum